The Wild Side

EXTREME SPORTS

Henry Billings
Melissa Billings

JAMESTOWN  PUBLISHERS

a division of NTC/CONTEMPORARY PUBLISHING GROUP
Lincolnwood, Illinois USA

ISBN 0–8092-9517-2

Published by Jamestown Publishers,
a division of NTC/Contemporary Publishing Group, Inc.
4255 West Touhy Avenue,
Lincolnwood (Chicago), Illinois 60712-1975, U.S.A.

00 01 02 03 04 VL 10 9 8 7 6 5 4 3 2 1

The Wild Side

EXTREME SPORTS

CONTENTS

UNIT THREE

To the Student

Sports are important to us in many ways. Participation in sports, whether individual or team activities, contributes to good health. Cooperative skills learned in team sports are applicable throughout life. Even as observers, we feel pride in those who represent us in competitions. Extreme sports, however, are a different matter. An extreme sportsperson is less interested in improving his or her body than in challenging it, pushing it to its limits. He or she is less interested in winning or losing than in overcoming fear and doing what others said couldn't be done. The pride that an extreme athlete feels is often beyond the understanding of the general public, which may see little point to the risks that extreme sports present. In extreme sports, you will discover a world of excitement and challenge that will impress and startle you.

How to Use This Book

About the Book.   *Extreme Sports* contains three units, each of which includes five lessons. Each lesson begins with an article about an unusual subject or event. The article is followed by a group of four reading comprehension exercises and three critical thinking exercises. The reading comprehension exercises will help you understand the article. The critical thinking exercises will help you think about what you have read and how it relates to your own experience.

   At the end of each lesson, you will also have the opportunity to give your personal response to some aspect of the article and then to assess how well you understood what you read.

The Sample Lesson.   Working through the sample lesson, the first lesson in the book, with your class or group will demonstrate how a lesson is organized. The sample lesson explains how to complete the exercises and score your answers. The correct answers for the sample exercises and sample scores are printed in lighter type. In some cases, explanations of the correct answers are given. The explanations will help you understand how to think through these question types.

   If you have any questions about how to complete the exercises or score them, this is the time to get the answers.

Working Through Each Lesson.   Begin each lesson by looking at the photographs and reading the captions. Before you read, predict what you think the article will be about. Then read the article.

   Sometimes your teacher may decide to time your reading. Timing helps you keep track of and increase your reading speed. If you have been timed, enter your reading time in the box at the end of the lesson. Then use the Words-per-Minute Table to find your reading speed, and record your speed on the Reading Speed graph at the end of the unit.

   Next complete the Reading Comprehension and Critical Thinking exercises. The directions for each exercise will tell you how to mark your answers. When you have finished all four Reading Comprehension exercises, use the answer key provided by your teacher to check your work. Follow the directions after each exercise to find your score. Record your Reading Comprehension scores on the graph at the end of each unit. Then check your answers to the Author's Approach, Summarizing and Paraphrasing, and Critical Thinking exercises. Fill in the Critical Thinking Chart at the end of each unit with your evaluation of your work and comments about your progress.

   At the end of each unit you will also complete a Compare and Contrast Chart. The completed chart will help you see what the articles have in common, and it will give you an opportunity to explore your own ideas about the events in the articles.

SAMPLE
LESSON

Street Luge: Fast, Fun,...Dangerous!

Going really fast is easy. Any top street luge racer can hit 60 miles per hour or more. The tricky part is slowing down. If you do it well, you can smile and race again. If not, that cracking sound you hear will be your bones!

2   Street luge racing is becoming more and more popular in the United States. It's a great test of speed and skill. But it's also very dangerous. The idea is to race down a hill while lying on a skateboard. The skateboard is

In street luge, riders lie on their backs on an extra-long skateboard, like this one, and speed feetfirst down city streets. Broken bones and scraped skin are an unavoidable part of this sport.

extra long, but it has no padding. And believe it or not, it has no brakes.

3   To race, street lugers lie down on the skateboards. They lie on their backs with their feet in front. That puts them just a few inches off the road. They steer by leaning to the left or the right. They have to know exactly how to position their bodies when heading into a curve. Turning too much or too little will send a skateboard flying off the course. It's no wonder street lugers are sometimes called pilots!

4   Street luge is not done on a special track. Instead, racers use regular streets. Although they wait until these streets have been closed to traffic, many hazards remain. Sidewalks, street signs, and telephone poles all pose threats to the racers. And that's not all. Some race courses have 90-degree turns in the middle. Any racer who fails to make the turn is bound to crash into something hard.

5   Stopping without brakes can be a real challenge. Racers must use their feet as brakes. They drag them hard on the asphalt. Often they dig in with such force that they leave skid marks.

They send smoke and the smell of burning rubber into the air.

6   Racers need some kind of protection for their bodies. They wear helmets, elbow pads, and leather clothing. Still, sooner or later anyone who races will get hurt. Bob Pereyra is a top street luger. He broke both ankles in one crash. In another accident, he broke three ribs. And in a bad practice run in 1995, he fractured a heel in three places. Roger Hickey is also a top racer. Over his career, he has broken more than 50 bones. He says he has also left enough skin on the road "to make a mannequin."

7   If the pros get this banged up, what happens to rookies? Darren Lott, author of *Street Luge Survival Guide,* writes about one young daredevil named Zac Bernstein. At the age of 21, Zac knew no fear. He took to street luge quickly. He wanted to go faster and faster on every run. On one steep hill, he took a turn a bit wide. He went bouncing into a field and hit a storm drain. He smashed right into the concrete wall on the far side of the drain.

8 Without his helmet, Zac would have died. Even with it, he broke lots of bones and slit open his throat. Zac spent weeks in the hospital recovering. But just one month after the accident, he was back racing again. He had pins in his hip and leg and walked with a cane. But he was not ready to give up the sport he loved.

9 Street luge has been around for years. No one person "invented" it. Instead, the sport caught on in several places more or less at the same time. Darren Lott writes, "In the 1970s we were constantly running into little groups that thought they were the only ones in the world doing it." That has changed. Today street luge is getting lots of attention. It has even shown up on TV sports shows. Still, as long as there are people like Zac Bernstein around, street luge will remain a truly extreme sport. 🦎

If you have been timed while reading this article, enter your reading time below. Then turn to the Words-per-Minute Table on page 55 and look up your reading speed (words per minute). Enter your reading speed on the graph on page 56.

Reading Time: Sample Lesson

——————— : ———————
Minutes   Seconds

A | Finding the Main Idea

One statement below expresses the main idea of the article. One statement is too general, or too broad. The other statement explains only part of the article; it is too narrow. Label the statements using the following key:

M—Main Idea   B—Too Broad   N—Too Narrow

___B___ 1. Street luge often results in injury to the athletes who take part in it. [This statement is *too broad*. It doesn't give a clear idea of the sport that the article is about.]

___M___ 2. Street luge racers, who speed down streets lying on long skateboards without brakes, love the sport despite frequent injuries. [This statement is the *main idea*. It describes what happens in street luge and how lugers feel about the sport.]

___N___ 3. Professional street luge racer Roger Hickey has broken more than 50 bones. [This statement is true but *too narrow*. It tells about only one detail mentioned in the article.]

___15___ Score 15 points for a correct M answer.

___10___ Score 5 points for each correct B or N answer.

___25___ **Total Score:** Finding the Main Idea

B | Recalling Facts

How well do you remember the facts in the article? Put an X in the box next to the answer that correctly completes each statement about the article.

1. Street luge racers can hit speeds
    ☒ a. of 60 miles per hour or more.
    ☐ b. between 40 and 50 miles per hour.
    ☐ c. of about 100 miles per hour.

2. Street luge racers steer their boards by
    ☐ a. dragging a foot on one side at a time.
    ☐ b. mental telepathy.
    ☒ c. shifting their bodies.

3. Preparations for a street luge race include
    ☐ a. removing all street signs that can be moved.
    ☒ b. closing the street to normal traffic.
    ☐ c. installing rubber bumpers along curbs.

4. Even pros like Roger Hickey
    ☐ a. replace their brakes after each race.
    ☐ b. avoid race courses with 90-degree turns.
    ☒ c. face the possibility of breaking many bones.

5. One proof of street luge's popularity is that
    ☒ a. TV sports shows have begun to cover street luge events.
    ☐ b. street luge has been around for years.
    ☐ c. those who participate love the sport.

Score 5 points for each correct answer.

___25___ **Total Score:** Recalling Facts

C Making Inferences

When you combine your own experience and information from a text to draw a conclusion that is not directly stated in that text, you are making an inference. Below are five statements that may or may not be inferences based on information in the article. Label the statements using the following key:

C—Correct Inference   **F—Faulty Inference**

___C___ 1. The way in which weight is arranged across a moving object affects the object's movement. [This is a *correct* inference. Paragraph 3 discusses how the racers position their bodies to steer their boards.]

___C___ 2. An early step in arranging a street luge race is notifying the local police department. [This is a *correct* inference. A street must be closed by local authorities before lugers may use it.]

___F___ 3. Street lugers do not spend much on gear. [This is a *faulty* inference. Lugers need their boards, leather clothing, helmets, special shoes, and additional padding.]

___F___ 4. Standard rules for street luge were decided on before the first races were held in the 1970s. [This is a *faulty* inference. At first many groups were doing street luge separately; rules were later standardized.]

___C___ 5. Street lugers will spend a great deal of time in hospitals and emergency rooms. [This is a *correct* inference.]

> Score 5 points for each correct answer.
>
> ___25___ **Total Score:** Making Inferences

D Using Words Precisely

Each numbered sentence below contains an underlined word or phrase from the article. Following the sentence are three definitions. One definition is closest to the meaning of the underlined word. One definition is opposite or nearly opposite. Label those two definitions using the following key; do not label the remaining definition.

C—Closest   **O—Opposite or Nearly Opposite**

1. They have to know exactly how to <u>position</u> their bodies when heading into a curve.

___C___ a. place

_____ b. count

___O___ c. randomly move

2. Although they wait until these streets have been closed to traffic, many <u>hazards</u> remain.

___O___ a. items that contribute to safety

___C___ b. dangers

_____ c. people

3. And in a bad practice run in 1995, he <u>fractured</u> a heel in three places.

_____ a. covered

___C___ b. broke

___O___ c. mended

4. Darren Lott, author of *Street Luge Survival Guide,* writes about one young <u>daredevil</u> named Zac Bernstein.

___C___ a. a person who takes chances and acts recklessly

_____ b. a person who plays sports for money

___O___ c. a person who is extremely careful

5. Street luge has been around for years. No one person "invented" it.

___C___ a. discovered

___O___ b. copied

_____ c. interrupted

___15___ Score 3 points for each correct C answer.

___10___ Score 2 points for each correct O answer.

___25___ **Total Score:** Using Words Precisely

Enter the four total scores in the spaces below, and add them together to find your Reading Comprehension Score. Then record your score on the graph on page 57.

Score	Question Type	Sample Lesson
25	Finding the Main Idea	
25	Recalling Facts	
25	Making Inferences	
25	Using Words Precisely	
100	**Reading Comprehension Score**	

Author's Approach

Put an X in the box next to the correct answer.

1. The main purpose of the first paragraph is to

☐ a. describe exactly how street luge is done.

☒ b. stress how dangerous street luge can be.

☐ c. persuade athletes to try street luge.

2. Judging by statements from the article "Street Luge: Fast, Fun, . . . Dangerous!" you can conclude that the authors want the reader to think that

☐ a. experienced street lugers never get hurt.

☐ b. it is easy to street luge safely.

☒ c. street lugers take risks every time they ride.

3. Choose the statement below that is the weakest argument for participating in street luge races.

☐ a. Street luge racing is fun.

☐ b. Street luge racing takes a lot of practice.

☒ c. Street luge racing can cause serious injuries.

4. How is the authors' purpose for writing the article expressed in paragraph 2?

☒ a. The paragraph describes street luge racing and states that the sport is both dangerous and popular.

☐ b. The paragraph describes the street luger's skateboard.

☐ c. The paragraph states that street luge racing is a test of skill.

___4___ Number of correct answers

Record your personal assessment of your work on the Critical Thinking Chart on page 58.

Summarizing and Paraphrasing

Follow the directions provided for question 1. Put an X in the box next to the correct answer for the other questions.

1. Look for the important ideas and events in paragraphs 7 and 8. Summarize those paragraphs in one or two sentences.

_____ Zac Bernstein, a rookie street luger, was badly hurt on a run. Even so,_____

_____ he returned to street luging just one month after his accident._____

_____

2. Below are summaries of the article. Choose the summary that says all the most important things about the article but in the fewest words.

☐ a. Even street lugers who wear protective gear—helmets, elbow pads, and leather clothing—have been injured in this fast-paced sport. [This summary mentions specific but unnecessary details and fails to tell what street luge is.]

☐ b. Street luging, a sport that requires balance, body control, and a love of speed, is becoming more popular. [This summary doesn't explain street luge or its dangers.]

☒ c. Street lugers lie down on skateboards and race down hills. Even though this sport has caused serious injuries, many athletes enjoy it so much that they continue to risk their lives by participating in it. [This summary says all the most important things about the article in the fewest words.]

3. Read the statement from the article below. Then read the paraphrase of that statement. Choose the reason that best tells why the paraphrase does not say the same thing as the statement.

Statement: Many race courses feature 90-degree turns that a skillful street luge racer must negotiate.

Paraphrase: Most race courses avoid right-angle turns that are difficult for racers to negotiate.

☐ a. Paraphrase says too much.

☐ b. Paraphrase doesn't say enough.

☒ c. Paraphrase doesn't agree with the statement. [This statement contradicts the first statement about 90-degree, or right-angle, turns.]

_____
| ___3___ Number of correct answers |

Record your personal assessment of your work on the Critical Thinking Chart on page 58.

Critical Thinking

Follow the directions provided for questions 1, 3, and 4. Put an X in the box next to the correct answer for the other questions.

1. For each statement below, write O if it expresses an opinion or write F if it expresses a fact.

___O___ a. Zac Bernstein should have stopped street luging after he had his terrible accident.

___F___ b. Street luging can be done on a city street.

___F___ c. Turning too much or too little will send the skateboard off the track.

2. Considering Zac Bernstein's actions as described in this article, you can predict that if he ever gives up street luging, he will probably

☐ a. find a safe sport to enjoy.

☐ b. refuse to participate in any other sport.

☒ c. take up another extreme sport.

CRITICAL THINKING

3. Choose from the letters below to correctly complete the following statement. Write the letters on the lines.

   On the positive side, ___b___, but on the negative side, ___a___.

   a. street luge racing is dangerous

   b. street luge racing is fun

   c. street luge racing has been around for years

4. Read paragraph 8. Then choose from the letters below to correctly complete the following statement. Write the letters on the lines.

   According to paragraph 8, ___a___ because ___c___.

   a. Zac Bernstein survived

   b. Zac Bernstein spent weeks in the hospital

   c. Zac Bernstein was wearing a helmet when he crashed

5. What did you have to do to answer question 2?

   ☐ a. make a prediction (what might happen next)

   ☒ b. find a cause (why something happened)

   ☐ c. find a contrast (how things are different)

   ___5___ Number of correct answers

   Record your personal assessment of your work on the Critical Thinking Chart on page 58.

Personal Response

What new question do you have about this topic?

___[After reading the article, you may have further questions about___

___street luging and the athletes who participate in it. Write one of___

___those questions on the lines.]___

_____

_____

Self-Assessment

I'm proud of my answer to question _____ in the _____ section because _____

___[Choose one answer from the exercises that you think you answered___

___particularly well. Tell why you are proud of either your answer or the___

___process by which you reached it.]___

_____

_____

Self-Assessment

To get the most out of the *Wild Side* series, you need to take charge of your own progress in improving your reading comprehension and critical thinking skills. Here are some of the features that help you work on those essential skills.

Reading Comprehension Exercises. Complete these exercises immediately after reading each article. They help you recall what you have read, understand the stated and implied main ideas, and add words to your working vocabulary.

Critical Thinking Skills Exercises. These exercises help you focus on the authors' approach and purpose, recognize and generate summaries and paraphrases, and identify relationships between ideas.

Personal Response and Self-Assessment. Questions in this category help you relate the articles to your personal experience and give you the opportunity to evaluate your understanding of the information in that lesson.

Compare and Contrast Charts. At the end of each unit you will complete a Compare and Contrast Chart. The completed chart helps you see what the articles have in common and gives you an opportunity to explore your own ideas about the topics discussed in the articles.

The Graphs. The graphs and charts at the end of each unit enable you to keep track of your progress. Check your graphs regularly with your teacher. Decide whether your progress is satisfactory or whether you need additional work on some skills. What types of exercises are you having difficulty with? Talk with your teacher about ways to work on the skills in which you need the most practice.

UNIT ONE

Snowboarding Out of Bounds

On March 7, 2000, Trevor Szold took a chance. He nearly paid for it with his life. Szold was snowboarding at Snow Valley Resort in California. But he didn't stay on the marked trails. Instead, he went off into the woods. A short time later he became lost. Szold didn't know which way to turn. The soft snow was five feet deep. "I was getting confused about what was the sky and what was the snow," he said. "Everything was white."

A snowboarder rides downhill like a surfer, standing with one foot ahead of the other on a single board. Snowboarding has much in common with surfing, skateboarding, and snow skiing. What sets it apart is its daredevil attitude—an attitude that can sometimes lead to trouble on the slopes.

2   Soon Szold grew tired and scared. He spent four cold nights in the woods. He drank water from a creek. Hunger drove him to eat spiders and insects. By the fourth day he had almost given up hope. "I was out of food and energy," Szold recalled. "I was concerned that I might die."

3   Luckily, a search team found him just in time. Szold had such a severe case of frostbite that he couldn't feel his hands or legs at all. His nose, fingers, and feet had swollen and turned black. "I'm just glad to be among the living," he said.

4   Snowboarding, like skiing, is a risky sport. Every year snowboarders (also called riders) and skiers get hurt. Broken bones are common. A few people even get killed. Mostly this is due to high speeds. People crash into each other or they hit a tree. Still, millions of people ski and ride without injury. In part that's because they play by the rules. They stay in bounds. They ride or ski only on designated trails. But for a few people, staying on the trails doesn't seem exciting enough. They go out of bounds, turning a risky sport into an extreme sport. Sometimes this leads to trouble.

5   In 1995 13-year-old Matt Archuleta and two other boys found that out. They wanted an extra thrill. So they snowboarded out of bounds at a ski resort in Idaho. At the end of their ride, they were far from the resort. The snow in the woods was too deep for them to hike through. So they dug a snow cave and spent a long, cold, scary night inside it. Like Szold, they were lucky. Searchers found them in time. "I'm not going to [snowboard out of bounds] again," said Archuleta. "We were really, really lucky."

6   Kevin Williamson and Shane Volkerding came much closer to death. You guessed it: they, too, rode out of bounds. They were making their last run of the day at a ski resort in Nevada. The weather was brutal. Blinding snow was falling and winds were whipping along at 40 miles per hour. It was hard to see more than a few feet.

7   The two men thought it might be less windy in the woods. So they left the trail. They believed they could stay close to it by boarding straight down the mountainside. They didn't know that the trail veered sharply away. So

by going straight they were really moving far away from the trail and safety. Also, the snow and wind turned out to be just as bad in the woods.

8   The men snowboarded quite a distance down the mountainside. At last, they reached a small riverbed. They couldn't ride any further. On all sides the land rose up around them. They had no choice but to take off their snowboards and start walking. But the snow was up to their waists. It was exhausting work. Soon Williamson and Volkerding were sopping wet from sweat. They struggled to the top of a ridge but couldn't see the ski resort.

9   As night came they used their snowboards to dig a cave. Although both men were wet and cold, they knew that somehow they had to stay warm. They huddled next to each other to share heat. They rubbed their feet. And they kept telling each other that they would be all right. Still, they had doubts. They thought about dying. Volkerding's mind began to play tricks on him. He thought he saw animals running within inches of his face.

10 At last morning came. The two men were rescued by a search team that had been looking for them since the middle of the night. Because Williamson and Volkerding had worked so hard to stay warm, they had no frostbite. "Many of these kinds of stories don't turn out nearly as well," said one official.

11 The story of Jeff Thornton certainly did not have a happy ending. No one knows if Thornton snowboarded out of bounds on purpose, but somehow this ninth grader ended up far off the trail. It was February 7, 1998, and Thornton was riding with his uncle at a California ski resort. When he went off the trail, he also lost sight of his uncle. The uncle later made it back to the ski resort. But the boy did not.

12 Thornton rode down into a riverbed. He became trapped. The weather couldn't have been worse. One blizzard after another swept through the region. Over the next few days, three feet of snow fell. The winds hit 70 miles per hour. Worse, the boy had no food. How long could he survive alone in the wilderness?

13 A massive search effort began. At one point there were 120 people looking for Thornton. Two helicopters were used. Two rescue dogs also helped out. But the heavy snow and high winds made it difficult for the searchers. Several days passed. Slowly, people gave up hope. No one thought Thornton could survive that long. After six days, he was given up for dead. The searchers began looking for a body.

14 At last, two searchers saw footprints in the snow. They followed them and found the boy. Amazingly, he was alive. "We saw him sitting on the bank of the creek," said one of the men. "He was just as surprised to see us as we were to see him."

15 Said one searcher, "How he survived the storms . . . I have no answer."

16 "I'm not sure if ever there was a more amazing rescue than this one," said another man.

17 The rescue seemed to come just in the nick of time. Within 10 minutes, fog moved in. That indicated a new storm was brewing.

18 Thornton seemed to be in pretty good shape. But looks were deceiving. He had frostbite on his legs, arms, and hands. He had broken bones. Also, he drank very little water during those six days in the woods. All these things took their toll on his body. Less than two weeks later, he had a heart attack and died. His death was a sober reminder of just how dangerous it can be to snowboard out of bounds.

If you have been timed while reading this article, enter your reading time below. Then turn to the Words-per-Minute table on page 55 and look up your reading speed (words per minute). Enter your reading speed on the graph on page 56.

Reading Time: Lesson 1

_____ : _____
Minutes   Seconds

A | Finding the Main Idea

One statement below expresses the main idea of the article. One statement is too general, or too broad. The other statement explains only part of the article; it is too narrow. Label the statements using the following key:

M—Main Idea   **B—Too Broad**   **N—Too Narrow**

_____ 1. Snowboarding off the trail may be exciting, but it may also lead to dire consequences.

_____ 2. Six days after ninth grader Jeff Thornton snowboarded out of bounds, he was rescued. At first, he looked fine, but he died soon after.

_____ 3. Following the rules is a good idea when it comes to a sport such as snowboarding.

_____ Score 15 points for a correct M answer.

_____ Score 5 points for each correct B or N answer.

_____ **Total Score**: Finding the Main Idea

B | Recalling Facts

How well do you remember the facts in the article? Put an X in the box next to the answer that correctly completes each statement about the article.

1. Some snowboarders stray from the marked trails because
   ☐ a. the trails are too difficult for them.
   ☐ b. they want more excitement.
   ☐ c. they are confused about where the trails are.

2. When Williamson and Volkerding got lost on a mountainside, they used their snowboards to
   ☐ a. dig a cave in the snow.
   ☐ b. signal for help.
   ☐ c. build a platform in tree branches.

3. Jeff Thornton snowboarded off the trail in
   ☐ a. California.
   ☐ b. Vermont.
   ☐ c. Colorado.

4. Rescuers found Thornton
   ☐ a. in a mountain cabin.
   ☐ b. by the side of a creek.
   ☐ c. in a cave.

5. Two weeks after being rescued, Thornton died of
   ☐ a. frostbite.
   ☐ b. complications from broken bones.
   ☐ c. a heart attack.

Score 5 points for each correct answer.

_____ **Total Score**: Recalling Facts

C | Making Inferences

When you combine your own experience with information from a text to draw a conclusion that is not directly stated in that text, you are making an inference. Below are five statements that may or may not be inferences based on information in the article. Label the statements using the following key:

C—Correct Inference   **F—Faulty Inference**

_____ 1. It is harder to maneuver a snowboard than it is to maneuver a pair of skis.

_____ 2. The worst danger that a person lost in the snow faces is frostbite.

_____ 3. People who run ski resorts do not want their guests to go off the marked trails.

_____ 4. Ski resorts in the western United States are more dangerous than those in the eastern part of the country.

_____ 5. Sometimes, even though searchers are convinced that a lost person is dead, they continue their search.

Score 5 points for each correct answer.

_____ **Total Score:** Making Inferences

D | Using Words Precisely

Each numbered sentence below contains an underlined word or phrase from the article. Following the sentence are three definitions. One definition is closest to the meaning of the underlined word. One definition is opposite or nearly opposite. Label those two definitions using the following key; do not label the remaining definition.

C—Closest   **O—Opposite or Nearly Opposite**

1. They didn't know that the trail <u>veered</u> sharply away.
_____ a. continued on a chosen path
___/___ b. changed direction
_____ c. flooded

2. They <u>huddled</u> next to each other to share heat.
_____ a. spoke
_____ b. kept a distance
_____ c. snuggled

3. That indicated a new storm was <u>brewing</u>.
_____ a. dying away
_____ b. strong
_____ c. developing

4. Thornton seemed to be in pretty good shape. But looks were <u>deceiving</u>.
_____ a. misleading
_____ b. surprising
_____ c. truthful

5. His death was a <u>sober</u> reminder of just how dangerous it can be to snowboard out of bounds.

_____ a. tardy

___/___ b. serious

_____ c. silly

_____ Score 3 points for each correct C answer.

_____ Score 2 points for each correct O answer.

_____ **Total Score:** Using Words Precisely

Enter the four total scores in the spaces below, and add them together to find your Reading Comprehension Score. Then record your score on the graph on page 57.

Score	Question Type	Lesson 1
_____	Finding the Main Idea	
_____	Recalling Facts	
_____	Making Inferences	
_____	Using Words Precisely	
_____	**Reading Comprehension Score**	

Author's Approach

Put an X in the box next to the correct answer.

1. What do the authors mean by the statement "[The snowboarders] didn't know that the trail veered sharply away. So by going straight they were really moving far away from the trail and safety"?

☐ a. The snowboarders were careless and reckless.

☐ b. An experienced snowboarder could have predicted that the trail would veer away.

☐ c. The snowboarders made an understandable error.

2. From the statements below, choose the one that you believe the authors would agree with.

☐ a. The fun that comes with going off the marked trails is worth the risk.

☐ b. Straying from the marked trails is a bad idea.

☐ c. Only adult snowboarders can leave the marked trails safely.

3. The authors tell this story mainly by

☐ a. telling different stories about the same topic.

☐ b. comparing different topics.

☐ c. using their imagination and creativity.

_____ Number of correct answers

Record your personal assessment of your work on the Critical Thinking Chart on page 58.

Summarizing and Paraphrasing

Follow the directions provided for question 1. Put an X in the box next to the correct answer for question 2.

1. Look for the important ideas and events in paragraphs 13 and 14. Summarize those paragraphs in one or two sentences.

_____

_____

_____

2. Choose the sentence that correctly restates the following sentence from the article: "When [Jeff Thornton] went off the trail, he also lost sight of his uncle."

☐ a. Thornton's uncle lost sight of him after he went off the trail.

☐ b. After going off the trail, Thornton could no longer see his uncle.

☐ c. Losing sight of his uncle made Thornton go off the trail.

_____ Number of correct answers

Record your personal assessment of your work on the Critical Thinking Chart on page 58.

Critical Thinking

Follow the directions provided for questions 1, 3, 4, and 5. Put an X in the box next to the correct answer for question 2.

1. For each statement below, write O if it expresses an opinion or write F if it expresses a fact.

_____ a. The fate of many snowboarders who chose to leave the marked trails should serve as a warning to others who are tempted to break the rules.

_____ b. Snowboarding is a risky sport.

_____ c. Helicopters, rescue dogs, and 120 people searched for Jeff Thornton.

2. From what Trevor Szold said, you can predict that he will

☐ a. always feel grateful to his rescuers.

☐ b. probably snowboard out of bounds again as soon as possible.

☐ c. start eating spiders and insects for fun.

3. Choose from the letters below to correctly complete the following statement. Write the letters on the lines.

On the positive side, _____, but on the negative side, _____.

a. Jeff Thornton died soon after being rescued

b. Jeff Thornton was finally rescued

c. Jeff Thornton was snowboarding with his uncle

4. Think about cause-effect relationships in the article. Fill in the blanks in the cause-effect chart, drawing from the letters below.

Cause	Effect
Matt Archuleta and his friends wanted an extra thrill.	_____
Two lost snowboarders knew they needed to stay warm.	_____
_____	Many snowboarders get hurt each year.

a. Snowboarders often crash into each other at high speed.

b. They snowboarded off the marked trail.

c. They shared body heat by staying close to each other.

5. Which paragraphs from the article provide evidence that supports your answers to question 4?

_____

_____

_____ Number of correct answers
Record your personal assessment of your work on the Critical Thinking Chart on page 58.

Personal Response

Describe a time when you took a chance and then regretted your decision.

_____

_____

_____

Self-Assessment

I'm proud of my answer to question _____ in the _____

section because _____

_____

_____

_____.

Bungee Jumping

Anyone can do it. But it helps to be a little crazy. The idea is simple enough. You climb a high tower or crane. Or perhaps you go up in a hot-air balloon. In any case, someone attaches a thick rubber band around your ankles. Then you leap out into the wild blue yonder. Your body plunges toward the earth below. Then, at the last moment, the rubber band stops you. This is not your day to die.

Look out below! From this bungee jumper's point of view, humans on the ground below are as tiny as ants. Bungee jumpers regularly enjoy falls of 150 feet before their bungee cords pull them back to avoid painful collisions with the ground.

2   The sport is called bungee jumping. It began long ago as a ritual on certain islands in the South Pacific. (These islands form the present-day country of Vanuatu.) Each spring the islanders gathered vines. They wove them into a kind of rope. Then young men called "land divers" climbed high towers. They tied the vines to their ankles and jumped. They did it to prove their courage. A good jump was also supposed to help ensure healthy crops for the island.

3   Modern bungee jumping began in England on April 1, 1979. Note the day. It was April Fool's Day. The members of the Oxford Dangerous Sports Club were looking for a new thrill. They had heard of "land diving" and wanted to try it for themselves. So the men climbed up a high bridge, tied rubber cords to their ankles, and jumped. One member later said the jump was "quite pleasurable, really."

4   But it was a man from New Zealand who made bungee jumping a big sport. His name was Alan John Hackett. Hackett was quite a daredevil. He had once jumped off the Eiffel Tower in Paris, France. Then, in 1988, he wanted to give others a chance to try bungee jumping. At that time, though, the sport was illegal. So Hackett made a deal with New Zealand police. Using his own money, he would fix up a dilapidated bridge over a river gorge. In return, the police would let him open a legal bungee jumping center on the bridge.

5   The center was a huge success. Hackett gave each jumper a special T-shirt. It became a hot item among daredevils. Everyone wanted one of those shirts. And since the only way to get one was to make a jump, more and more people agreed to do it. Some jumpers did really wild things. They asked to jump with an extra-long cord. That way they would dip into the river before the cord pulled them back. One man put shampoo on his head. When he bounced up out of the water, he was washing his hair!

6   Bungee jumping soon caught on in the United States. It was introduced in California and Colorado. Then it spread to other states. At first, only the boldest people did it. But over time, others joined in. All kinds of people took the plunge. Even one man who was helped out of a wheelchair jumped. And no jumpers complained about paying $50 or more to do it.

7   As thrills go, it's hard to beat bungee jumping. The platforms used for the jumps are 10 stories high—or higher. That means jumpers fall as far as 150 feet before the cord saves them. First-time jumpers can almost taste their fear. Jay Petrow thought about it for a year before he jumped. He said his palms began to sweat just thinking about it. Emily Trask said, "The first time I jumped, I was terrified." Nora Jacobson said, "My terror [was] cold and rippling."

8   Some jumpers use humor to calm their nerves. Just before her first jump, a woman named Alison was asked how old she was. "I hope to be 29 soon," she replied. Most jumpers are young, but some are not. S. L. Potter made his first leap at the age of 100. "It was now or never," he later explained.

9   There is, of course, real danger. There is no margin for error in bungee jumping. One mistake, and you're history. And while most people live to tell the tale, a few don't. In 1989 two French jumpers died when their cords

broke. A third died when he slammed into a tower. In 1991 Hal Irish became the first American jumper to die. Somehow his cord became detached as he dove through the air.

10 So accidents *do* happen. But for many, the danger just adds to the excitement. Besides, bungee jumpers don't talk about the tragedies. They talk about the triumphs. They talk about facing their fears. And they talk about the joy of the fall itself. During a jump, a person hits speeds of 60 miles an hour. Then, when the cord tightens, the jumper springs back up into the air like a rocket. For a short time, he or she is a kind of human yo-yo, bouncing up and down in the breeze. When the cord loses its bounce, the ride is over.

11 Even then, though, some of the joy remains. Jumpers feel both happy and relieved when it's over. Most laugh and smile as they are unhooked from the cord. "Hey, look at me! I did it!" many of them shout. It is, as one person said, "a natural high." Bungee jumpers even have a name for this soaring feeling. They call it the post-bungee grin. Maybe someday you'll decide to make that leap of faith and share that grin. All it takes is a little money—and a lot of nerve.

If you have been timed while reading this article, enter your reading time below. Then turn to the Words-per-Minute table on page 55 and look up your reading speed (words per minute). Enter your reading speed on the graph on page 56.

Reading Time: Lesson 2

_____ : _____
Minutes   *Seconds*

A Finding the Main Idea

One statement below expresses the main idea of the article. One statement is too general, or too broad. The other statement explains only part of the article; it is too narrow. Label the statements using the following key:

M—Main Idea   **B—Too Broad**   **N—Too Narrow**

_____ 1. Thousands of bungee jumpers have leaped from heights at the end of a strong rubber band both to enjoy flying through the air and to prove courage.

_____ 2. Of the thousands of people who have done bungee jumping, perhaps the oldest is S. L. Potter, who made his first leap at the age of 100.

_____ 3. Although it is based on a long-standing tradition in certain South Pacific islands, bungee jumping has acquired worldwide popularity only recently.

_____ Score 15 points for a correct M answer.

_____ Score 5 points for each correct B or N answer.

_____ **Total Score:** Finding the Main Idea

B Recalling Facts

How well do you remember the facts in the article? Put an X in the box next to the answer that correctly completes each statement about the article.

1. "Land divers" in Vanuatu depended on
   - ☐ a. thick rubber bands tied to their ankles.
   - ☐ b. cords made of vines tied to their ankles.
   - ☐ c. ropes made of leather tied to their ankles.

2. Members of the Oxford Dangerous Sports Club
   - ☐ a. made their famous dive in Vanuatu.
   - ☐ b. jumped from London Bridge.
   - ☐ c. started bungee jumping on April 1, 1979.

3. Bungee promoter Alan John Hackett was from
   - ☐ a. New Zealand.
   - ☐ b. California.
   - ☐ c. England.

4. To get Hackett's special T-shirts, people jumped
   - ☐ a. off a bridge.
   - ☐ b. off the Eiffel Tower.
   - ☐ c. out of a hot-air balloon.

5. The term _post-bungee grin_ refers to the
   - ☐ a. smile with which bungee jumpers recall long-past jumps.
   - ☐ b. happy face on Hackett's T-shirts.
   - ☐ c. feeling of joy and pride one feels immediately after bungee jumping.

Score 5 points for each correct answer.

_____ **Total Score:** Recalling Facts

C Making Inferences

When you combine your own experience and information from a text to draw a conclusion that is not directly stated in that text, you are making an inference. Below are five statements that may or may not be inferences based on information in the article. Label the statements using the following key:

C—Correct Inference　　　**F—Faulty Inference**

_____ 1. The people of Vanuatu would think bungee jumpers are courageous.

_____ 2. In 1979 members of the Oxford Dangerous Sports Club were sure that bungee jumping would become a popular sport within a short time.

_____ 3. Before 1988 New Zealand authorities considered bungee jumping a threat to public safety.

_____ 4. Bungee jumping requires that the jumper have a great deal of physical strength.

_____ 5. Bungee jumping is clearly more dangerous than riding a motorcycle without a helmet.

Score 5 points for each correct answer.

_____ **Total Score:** Making Inferences

D Using Words Precisely

Each numbered sentence below contains an underlined word or phrase from the article. Following the sentence are three definitions. One definition is closest to the meaning of the underlined word. One definition is opposite or nearly opposite. Label those two definitions using the following key; do not label the remaining definition.

C—Closest　　　**O—Opposite or Nearly Opposite**

1. It began long ago as a ritual on certain islands in the South Pacific.

_____ a. celebration

_____ b. formal, traditional event

_____ c. unplanned, disorganized event

2. A good jump was also supposed to help ensure healthy crops for the island.

_____ a. guarantee

_____ b. make well known

_____ c. reduce the chances of

3. One member later said the jump was "quite pleasurable, really."

_____ a. fast-moving

_____ b. unpleasant

_____ c. enjoyable

4. Then, in 1988, he wanted to give others a chance to try bungee jumping. At that time, though, the sport was illegal.

_____ a. lawful

_____ b. not understood

_____ c. against the law

5. Using his own money, he would fix up a <u>dilapidated</u> bridge over a river gorge.

_____ a. shabby

_____ b. new and attractive

_____ c. out-of-the-way

_____ Score 3 points for each correct C answer.

_____ Score 2 points for each correct A or D answer.

_____ **Total Score:** Using Words Precisely

Enter the four total scores in the spaces below, and add them together to find your Reading Comprehension Score. Then record your score on the graph on page 57.

Score	Question Type	Lesson 2
_____	Finding the Main Idea	
_____	Recalling Facts	
_____	Making Inferences	
_____	Using Words Precisely	
_____	**Reading Comprehension Score**	

Author's Approach

Put an X in the box next to the correct answer.

1. What is the authors' purpose in writing "Bungee Jumping"?

☐ a. to encourage the reader to try bungee jumping

☐ b. to inform the reader about bungee jumping

☐ c. to express an opinion against bungee jumping

2. Which of the following statements from the article best describes Alan John Hackett?

☐ a. Hackett was quite a daredevil.

☐ b. Hackett gave each jumper a special T-shirt.

☐ c. So Hackett made a deal with New Zealand police.

3. What do the authors imply by saying "Even one man who was helped out of a wheelchair jumped"?

☐ a. This man did not really want to jump; he was forced into it.

☐ b. Because he did not have full use of his legs, this man was taking a foolish risk by jumping.

☐ c. Bungee jumping doesn't demand that participants be in perfect physical condition.

4. The authors tells this story mainly by

☐ a. comparing different topics.

☐ b. telling different stories about the same topic.

☐ c. using his or her imagination and creativity.

_____ Number of correct answers

Record your personal assessment of your work on the Critical Thinking Chart on page 58.

Summarizing and Paraphrasing

Follow the directions provided for questions 1 and 2. Put an X in the box next to the correct answer for question 3.

1. Complete the following one-sentence summary of the article using the lettered phrases from the phrase bank below. Write the letters on the lines.

> **Phrase Bank**
> a. the popularity of bungee jumping in the United States
> b. a description of the feelings jumpers feel after they complete a jump
> c. the origins, or beginnings, of bungee jumping

The article "Bungee Jumping" begins with _____, goes on

to explain _____, and ends with _____.

2. Reread paragraph 9 in the article. Below, write a summary of the paragraph in no more than 25 words.

_____

_____

_____

_____

Reread your summary and decide whether it covers the important ideas in the paragraph. Next, decide how to shorten the summary to 15 words or less without leaving out any essential information. Write this summary below.

_____

_____

_____

3. Choose the sentence that correctly restates the following sentence from the article: "Using his own money, he would fix up a dilapidated bridge over a river gorge."

☐ a. He would find a rickety bridge over a river and repair it by himself.

☐ b. With his own money, he would build a new bridge to replace the old one over a river.

☐ c. He would spend his own money to repair an old, dangerous bridge over a river gorge.

> _____ Number of correct answers
>
> Record your personal assessment of your work on the Critical Thinking Chart on page 58.

Critical Thinking

Follow the directions provided for questions 1 and 5. Put an X in the box next to the correct answer for the other questions.

1. For each statement below, write *O* if it expresses an opinion or write *F* if it expresses a fact.

_____ a. Bungee jumping was first introduced to the United States in California and Colorado.

_____ b. Bungee jumping should be declared illegal, since it is so risky.

_____ c. Modern bungee jumping began on April 1, 1979.

2. From what the article said about the popularity of bungee jumping, you can predict that

☐ a. within five years, everyone in the world will have tried the sport.

☐ b. the sport will stay popular for a while.

☐ c. everyone will soon give up the sport because it is too dangerous.

3. What was the cause of the jumps by early land divers in the South Pacific?

☐ a. The local law demanded that every young man jump off high towers.

☐ b. The men wanted to become taller and thought that land diving would be an efficient way to stretch their legs.

☐ c. The men wanted to prove their courage.

4. How is "Bungee Jumping" related to the theme of *Extreme Sports*?

☐ a. Bungee jumping is an old sport.

☐ b. Bungee jumping is an unusual sport that demands a special willingness to take risks.

☐ c. Bungee jumping is popular around the world today.

5. In which paragraph did you find your information or details to answer question 3? _____

_____ Number of correct answers

Record your personal assessment of your work on the Critical Thinking Chart on page 58.

Personal Response

What new question do you have about this topic?

_____

_____

_____

_____

Self-Assessment

Before reading this article, I already knew _____

_____

_____

_____

_____

White-Water Thrills

You can go to Disney World and ride Splash Mountain. It's safe and lots of fun. But Splash Mountain is the same ride over and over again. If you want to try something different, try white-water rafting. A white-water ride is never the same twice. New thrills and dangers lie downstream every time you "run the rapids."

2   *White water* means "river rapids." The water becomes a foamy "white" when it swirls over and around rocks. All rapids are called white water. But not all white-water rivers are the same. Some are pretty tame; others are really

White foam shooting up out of swirling waters all around you . . . beyond the water, high cliffs rising at both sides . . . jagged rocks jutting up out of the water . . . and pressing in on you, the roar of the rapids and the rushing wind—you are white-water rafting!

wild. Rafters need to know what they are facing. A gentle-looking river can turn into a beast around the next bend. So all rivers are rated based on how hard they are to travel down.

3   The most common rating system uses Roman numerals from I to VI. A Class I river is wide with a few small waves. It's not much more exciting than a splash in an old bathtub. A Class III river is much more difficult. It has rocks and waves up to three feet high. You can expect to get wet running the rapids of a Class III river.

4   If you move up to a Class V river, you will face violent rapids with no breaks. You can get killed on a Class V river. A Class VI river is even worse. It's a real hair-raiser. All kinds of dangers await you there. Anyone who takes on a Class VI river must be two things—an expert and a daredevil. A few rivers have sections that are off the scale. These "Class VII" rivers can't be rafted by anyone.

5   Rivers change all the time. A heavy rain can turn a Class III river into a Class V or even a Class VI. Some rivers can be run only in the spring after the snow melts. The rest

of the time there just isn't enough water in them.

6   Rivers are like magnets for thrill seekers. Some people run the rapids in canoes. Others use one-person kayaks. Still others choose 16-foot rubber rafts. The rafts have one big advantage. They can stay afloat on rivers that would swamp a canoe or kayak.

7   One of the top 10 white-water rivers in the world is the Gauley River. It runs through West Virginia. The Gauley is a rafter's dream . . . or—if you're not careful—a nightmare. It has 28 miles of heart-pounding rapids. Each set of rapids has its own name. Some give fair warning to rafters. One is called Pure Screaming Hell. There are also Lost Paddle, Heaven Help Us, and Pillow Rock. River guide Roger Harrison describes Pillow Rock this way: "[It's] 15 seconds of uncontrolled violence."

8   Clearly, white-water rafting is not for the meek. Dangers lurk everywhere. There is, for example, something called a "keeper." A keeper is a kind of whirlpool. It is created when water rushes over a huge rock with a steep face. A keeper has enough

water power to trap, or keep, a boat for days. Imagine what it could do to a person! Keepers cause more drownings than any other hazard.

9   There are other pitfalls as well. There are waterfalls, fallen tree limbs, and sharp boulders. Any one of these can spell disaster. And no rafter wants to be caught in a "Colorado sandwich." That can happen when a raft hits a big wave. The front and back of the raft are folded up toward the center. Anyone in the middle is lunch meat in a raft sandwich.

10   Most rafters know the risks. And they are willing to take them. But they also do what they can to cut down the dangers. They carry at least 50 feet of strong rope for towing. They often wear wet suits and life jackets in case they get flipped into the water. And they wear helmets in case they hit a rock when they're dumped overboard.

11   Rafters also wear waterproof shoes. Some rookies want to take their shoes off as soon as they get wet. Wet shoes are uncomfortable. And rookies worry that wearing shoes will make it harder to swim if they're dumped into the water. But taking off their shoes would be a mistake. Shoes offer rafters' feet their only protection from rocks.

12   Look at it this way: if you end up in the river, you can't swim anyway. The current is just too strong. All you can do is float on your back with your feet pointed down the river. You'll need your feet to help steer around the rocks. If you're wearing shoes, your feet won't get cut up too badly. And when you finally reach the shore, you'll be glad you're wearing shoes. It might be a long walk home over very rocky ground!

13   Every year, thousands of people enjoy white-water rafting. But once in a while, the sport turns deadly. That happened in the summer of 1987. There were four accidents in British Columbia. Twelve rafters died in the span of eight weeks. The rivers in that part of Canada are snow-fed. They are very cold. Five of the dead rafters were American businessmen looking for a thrill. On August 1, they took on the wild Chilko River without wet suits.

A huge wave knocked them out of their raft. The men died in the frigid water.

14   So to enjoy the sport, you *must* respect the power of the river. That means playing it as safe as possible. But no extreme sport is completely safe. Dave Arnold owns a rafting company on the Gauley River. He warns his customers about the potential risks. Arnold and his guides are cautious. They make sure people know what they are doing. As Arnold puts it, "We never say rafting is safe." 🐉

If you have been timed while reading this article, enter your reading time below. Then turn to the Words-per-Minute table on page 55 and look up your reading speed (words per minute). Enter your reading speed on the graph on page 56.

Reading Time: Lesson 3

_____ : _____
Minutes   Seconds

A | Finding the Main Idea

One statement below expresses the main idea of the article. One statement is too general, or too broad. The other statement explains only part of the article; it is too narrow. Label the statements using the following key:

M—Main Idea **B—Too Broad** **N—Too Narrow**

_____ 1. Rivers are rated using Roman numerals from I to VI, depending on how hard they are to travel down.

_____ 2. White-water rafting is a sport that offers excitement and thrills.

_____ 3. While it offers fun and excitement, white-water rafting requires careful planning and an awareness of its risks.

_____ Score 15 points for a correct M answer.

_____ Score 5 points for each correct B or N answer.

_____ **Total Score:** Finding the Main Idea

B | Recalling Facts

How well do you remember the facts in the article? Put an X in the box next to the answer that correctly completes each statement about the article.

1. A Class I river
   ☐ a. has rocks and waves up to three feet high.
   ☐ b. has violent rapids with no breaks.
   ☐ c. is wide with a few small waves.

2. A Class III river can turn into a Class V river if
   ☐ a. a heavy rain falls.
   ☐ b. no rain falls for weeks.
   ☐ c. you are not an experienced rafter.

3. One danger, known as a "keeper," is a
   ☐ a. whirlpool that holds a boat underwater.
   ☐ b. big wave that can sink a raft.
   ☐ c. fallen tree limb that can put a hole in a raft.

4. It's a good idea to wear shoes in a raft because
   ☐ a. your feet get uncomfortable if they get wet.
   ☐ b. wearing shoes helps you steer the raft.
   ☐ c. shoes will protect your feet from rocks if you end up in the river.

5. Some rivers in British Columbia are dangerously cold because they are
   ☐ a. so far north.
   ☐ b. fed by melting snow.
   ☐ c. very deep.

Score 5 points for each correct answer.

_____ **Total Score:** Recalling Facts

C Making Inferences

When you combine your own experience and information from a text to draw a conclusion that is not directly stated in that text, you are making an inference. Below are five statements that may or may not be inferences based on information in the article. Label the statements using the following key:

C—Correct Inference   F—Faulty Inference

_____ 1. Wet suits keep swimmers in cold water much warmer than ordinary clothing does.

_____ 2. You would be foolish to attempt to raft a Class VII river.

_____ 3. It would be wise to run the Gauley River in a canoe rather than a raft.

_____ 4. If you take a camera down the river, you should make sure that it is waterproof.

_____ 5. The dangers of white-water rafting make it an unpopular sport with almost everyone.

Score 5 points for each correct C or F answer.

_____ **Total Score:** Making Inferences

D Using Words Precisely

Each numbered sentence below contains an underlined word or phrase from the article. Following the sentence are three definitions. One definition is closest to the meaning of the underlined word. One definition is opposite or nearly opposite. Label those two definitions using the following key; do not label the remaining definition.

C—Closest   O—Opposite or Nearly Opposite

1. Some <u>rookies</u> want to take their shoes off as soon as they get wet.

_____ a. rafters

_____ b. beginners

_____ c. people with experience

2. They can stay afloat on rivers that would <u>swamp</u> a canoe or kayak.

_____ a. dry out

_____ b. light

_____ c. fill with water

3. Clearly, white-water rafting is not for the <u>meek</u>.

_____ a. timid

_____ b. bold and daring

_____ c. elderly

4. There are other <u>pitfalls</u> as well. There are waterfalls, fallen tree limbs, and sharp boulders.

_____ a. sights

_____ b. benefits

_____ c. hidden dangers

5. He warns his customers about the <u>potential</u> risks.

_____ a. likely

_____ b. many

_____ c. impossible

_____ Score 3 points for each correct C answer.

_____ Score 2 points for each correct O answer.

_____ **Total Score:** Using Words Precisely

Enter the four total scores in the spaces below, and add them together to find your Reading Comprehension Score. Then record your score on the graph on page 57.

Score	Question Type	Lesson 3
_____	Finding the Main Idea	
_____	Recalling Facts	
_____	Making Inferences	
_____	Using Words Precisely	
_____	**Reading Comprehension Score**	

Author's Approach

Put an X in the box next to the correct answer.

1. What do the authors mean by the statement "A Class I river is wide with a few small waves"?

☐ a. A Class I river is safe and easy to travel down.

☐ b. A Class I river is too boring for any rafter to bother with.

☐ c. A Class I river is the only kind of river suitable for rafting.

2. From the statements below, choose those that you believe the authors would agree with.

☐ a. Even experienced rafters are terrified each time they go white-water rafting.

☐ b. Even experienced rafters must respect the power and danger of a fast-moving river.

☐ c. Experienced rafters can be certain they will be safe when they white-water raft.

3. The authors probably wrote this article to

☐ a. create a mood of excitement.

☐ b. discourage readers from white-water rafting.

☐ c. inform readers about white-water rafting.

_____ Number of correct answers

Record your personal assessment of your work on the Critical Thinking Chart on page 58.

Summarizing and Paraphrasing

Follow the directions provided for question 1. Put an X in the box next to the correct answer for the other questions.

1. Look for the important ideas and events in paragraphs 11 and 12. Summarize those paragraphs in one or two sentences.

    _____

    _____

    _____

2. Below are summaries of the article. Choose the summary that says all the most important things about the article but in the fewest words.

    ☐ a. Thrillseekers enjoy the sometimes dangerous sport of running the rapids in canoes, kayaks, and rafts. Rivers are classified according to their difficulty to travel down so people don't attempt a river beyond their abilities. Even so, accidents happen and rafters can become injured or even die.

    ☐ b. The sport of white-water rafting demands courage and skill. To do it successfully, you must reduce your risks by using the proper equipment, such as wet suits, helmets, and waterproof shoes.

    ☐ c. The Gauley River in West Virginia has many areas where a white-water rafter can get into trouble. Rafters must respect the power of the river if they want to survive their trips.

3. Choose the best one-sentence paraphrase for the following sentence from the article: "All you can do is float on your back with your feet pointed down the river."

    ☐ a. Your only choice is to float down the river feet first.

    ☐ b. One option you may want to try is to float on your back with your feet pointed.

    ☐ c. If your feet are pointed down the river, you will be able to float.

_____ Number of correct answers

Record your personal assessment of your work on the Critical Thinking Chart on page 58.

Critical Thinking

Put an X in the box next to the correct answer for questions 1, 4, and 5. Follow the directions provided for the other questions.

1. From the article, you can predict that if an inexperienced rafter tried to go down a Class VII river alone, he or she

    ☐ a. would most likely run into serious trouble or even die.

    ☐ b. could travel safely by using a few common-sense precautions.

    ☐ c. could relax and enjoy the trip.

2. Choose from the letters below to correctly complete the following statement. Write the letters on the lines.

In the article, the fate of _____ and the fate of _____ are alike.

   a. five American businessmen on the Chilko River

   b. rafting-company owner Dave Arnold

   c. of river guide Roger Harrison

3. Choose from the letters below to correctly complete the following statement. Write the letters on the lines.

According to the article,_____ caused rafters to _____,

and the effect was _____.

   a. a huge wave

   b. the rafters died

   c. fall out of the raft into frigid water

4. If you were a river guide, how could you use the information in the article to keep your customers safe?

   ☐ a. Discourage inexperienced rafters from trying to go down Class VI rivers.

   ☐ b. Advise the rafters to take their shoes off if they become uncomfortable.

   ☐ c. Outfit the rafters in wet suits, helmets, and waterproof shoes.

5. What did you have to do to answer question 2?

   ☐ a. find a description (how something looks)

   ☐ b. find a comparison (how things are the same)

   ☐ c. find a cause (why something happened)

_____ Number of correct answers

Record your personal assessment of your work on the Critical Thinking Chart on page 58.

Personal Response

How do you think you would feel if you were thrown from a raft into a fast-moving white-water river?

_____

_____

_____

Self-Assessment

From reading this article, I have learned _____

_____

_____

_____

CRITICAL THINKING

37

Hang Gliding

It all started one day back in the 1960s. Water-skier Bill Moyes tied a long kite to the back of a motorboat. He attached himself to the kite with a harness. Then he motioned for the motorboat to take off. Moments later, the speeding boat pulled the kite—and Moyes—high up into the air.

2   It was a great ride. Moyes looked down at the sparkling water far below. He soared soundlessly through the air, feeling almost like a bird. The plan was for the boat driver to slow the boat down gradually. That would cause Moyes to sink back to Earth. But all at once, Moyes spotted trouble ahead. The motorboat was pulling him right toward some high-tension wires! At that point Moyes did the only thing he could think of: he released the rope that tied him to the boat.

3   Suddenly, Moyes truly was flying like a bird. He was no longer connected to anything on the ground. The wings of the kite kept him from plummeting. They caught the wind and allowed him to glide gently down to earth. And so he completed the world's first hang gliding journey.

4   From then on, Moyes was hooked. He made lots of flights with his "wings" strapped on. He stopped using a motorboat to get into the air. Instead, he just climbed to the top of a ledge or cliff and jumped off. In 1970 he even soared over the Grand Canyon. Others began following his lead. Like Moyes, they used kites with flexible wings. They also figured out how to steer by shifting their weight back and forth.

5   When hang gliding "pilots" take off, they may plunge through the air in a free fall for 10 or 20 feet. Then their wings catch air currents and they begin to rise. By gliding from current to current, hang gliding pilots can float among the clouds for hours. They can make their gliders do loops, dives, and turns. And they can land with pinpoint accuracy.

6   These pilots make it look easy. And in some ways, it is. There's no motor to worry about. There are no complicated instruments. It's just you, your wings, and the wind. It is, says one pilot, "the closest approach man has to pure flight."

7   But hang gliding has a darker side. It can be dangerous. In fact, it can be downright deadly. More than one pilot has died while trying to navigate a glider. Many others have been badly hurt. In 1993, 29-year-old Leonard Stabb went hang gliding in the mountains of New York. There was very little wind that day. So Stabb decided to add some excitement to his flight. He steered his glider near some trees, but he got too close. He smashed into a tree. He was so badly injured

Did you ever wish you could float on the breeze? You may want to try hang gliding. One pilot described the experience this way: "You really feel like a bird. You feel the wind on you and the flutter of the sail." Here, a pilot glides over the ocean in an evening flight.

that doctors were not sure he would live. Stabb did live, but he never fully recovered from the accident.

8 Bob Abbott was even less fortunate. He was hang gliding in New Mexico in 1981. For a while, he sailed smoothly through the air. Then winds began to carry him toward some storm clouds. Abbott found his peaceful ride becoming rockier. Soon he found himself in the middle of a thunderstorm. He tried to fight his way through it. But the storm was too intense. The glider crashed. The 26-old Abbott did not survive.

9 Clearly, thunderstorms and trees are big dangers. But there are others as well. Pilots must be careful not to take off in winds that are too high. They have to be especially careful to avoid "rotors." Those are strong winds that come rolling in off mountains. Rotors can cut through a regular wind current and send the glider spinning out of control. They can cause a glider to take a nosedive straight down. That's called "going over the falls."

10 Sometimes, when pilots go over the falls, they can steady the glider and bring it safely out of the dive. But sometimes they can't. Then even the best pilots have to bail out. In the 1993 World Hang Gliding Championships, top pilot Brad Koji went over the falls. As he did so, his body slammed into the wings of his glider. Luckily, Koji was wearing a parachute. He was able to open his chute and float 14,000 feet back to earth.

11 Pilots also have to be on the lookout for "dust devils." These are tight swirls of air that lift sand, dirt, and bits of litter off the ground. They can also lift up a glider. Italian pilot Andrea Noseda was caught in a dust devil in 1993. Noseda's glider was pulled up into the air then smashed back to the ground. Noseda broke three bones in the crash.

12 At times, pilots seem to be asking for trouble. They pick takeoff points that add to the risks. For instance, some hang gliding pilots jump off from Dead Horse Point. That is a 2,000-foot sandstone cliff in Utah. At the bottom of the cliff lie a cactus or two—and a whole bunch of jagged rocks. As one man put it, "If you make a mistake going off this cliff, you're dead." When Reggie Jones peered over Dead Horse Point for the first time, he felt his stomach turn to knots. "I can't do it," he blurted out. "I can't jump."

13 Jones did jump, but he is not the only one to have felt that kind of terror. Many people have struggled to control their panic just before takeoff. As one pilot put it, "It's the fear. It's most intense before you launch. Then it's OK."

14 In fact, once you're in the air, the ride is much more than simply "OK."

It is fantastic. Pilots say they feel great joy as they soar high above the earth. Dave Kilbourne put it this way: "You're out in the open with nothing around you; sometimes you forget you even have a kite." Said Karen Rowley, "You really feel like a bird. You feel the wind on you and the flutter of the sail. It really is like you're a part of [the glider itself]." It is that thrill—the thrill of flying free— that makes hang gliding so appealing. Many pilots feel a special bond with the birds they meet in the sky. Reggie Jones knows that feeling. "I used to be a duck hunter," he said. "But ever since I started gliding, I haven't been able to kill a bird."

If you have been timed while reading this article, enter your reading time below. Then turn to the Words-per-Minute table on page 55 and look up your reading speed (words per minute). Enter your reading speed on the graph on page 56.

Reading Time: Lesson 4

_____ : _____
Minutes   Seconds

A | Finding the Main Idea

One statement below expresses the main idea of the article. One statement is too general, or too broad. The other statement explains only part of the article; it is too narrow. Label the statements using the following key:

M—Main Idea   **B—Too Broad**   **N—Too Narrow**

_____ 1. Strong winds can spell disaster for hang gliders, as one rider discovered when he was carried into a thunderstorm.

_____ 2. Hang gliding requires skill as well as the proper equipment.

_____ 3. Hang gliders, who float through the air attached to kites with wings, come as close to flying like birds as human beings can.

_____ Score 15 points for a correct M answer.

_____ Score 5 points for each correct B or N answer.

_____ **Total Score:** Finding the Main Idea

B | Recalling Facts

How well do you remember the facts in the article? Put an X in the box next to the answer that correctly completes each statement about the article.

1. The first time he hang glided, Bill Moyes released the tow rope so he could avoid
   ☐ a. high-tension wires.
   ☐ b. a large ship coming his way.
   ☐ c. another water-skier.

2. Kite wings are important because they
   ☐ a. protect the pilot from rain and wind.
   ☐ b. remind the pilot of birds' wings.
   ☐ c. catch air currents and lift the kite.

3. Pilots must watch out for "rotors," which are
   ☐ a. nearby airplanes.
   ☐ b. strong winds that roll off mountains.
   ☐ c. radio and TV antennae.

4. When pilots "go over the falls," it means that they
   ☐ a. fall rapidly.
   ☐ b. fly into a body of water.
   ☐ c. give up hang gliding.

5. Reggie Jones doesn't hunt ducks anymore because he
   ☐ a. is afraid that someday he will mistake a hang glider for a duck and will shoot its pilot.
   ☐ b. feels a special bond with birds now.
   ☐ c. wants to observe ducks flying.

Score 5 points for each correct answer.

_____ **Total Score:** Recalling Facts

C | Making Inferences

When you combine your own experience and information from a text to draw a conclusion that is not directly stated in that text, you are making an inference. Below are five statements that may or may not be inferences based on information in the article. Label the statements using the following key:

C—Correct Inference   **F—Faulty Inference**

_____ 1. Hang glider pilots should check the weather forecast before they take off.

_____ 2. Unlike airplane flying, hang gliding is always done within a few hundred feet of the earth.

_____ 3. People who hang glide are the only athletes to feel frightened before they participate in their sport.

_____ 4. Bill Moyes had not been at all interested in sports before he started hang gliding.

_____ 5. Hang glider pilots have less control of their vehicles than airplane pilots have of theirs.

> Score 5 points for each correct answer.
>
> _____ **Total Score:** Making Inferences

D | Using Words Precisely

Each numbered sentence below contains an underlined word or phrase from the article. Following the sentence are three definitions. One definition is closest to the meaning of the underlined word. One definition is opposite or nearly opposite. Label those two definitions using the following key; do not label the remaining definition.

C—Closest   **O—Opposite or Nearly Opposite**

1. The plan was for the boat driver to slow the boat down <u>gradually</u>.

_____ a. a little at a time

_____ b. all at once

_____ c. kindly

2. The wings of the kite kept him from <u>plummeting</u>.

_____ a. carrying

_____ b. falling suddenly

_____ c. rising slowly

3. Like Moyes, they used kites with <u>flexible</u> wings.

_____ a. bendable

_____ b. plastic

_____ c. stiff

4. There are no <u>complicated</u> instruments.

_____ a. favorite

_____ b. simple

_____ c. difficult to understand

5. More than one pilot has died while trying to <u>navigate</u> a glider.

_____ a. move without a set direction

_____ b. land

_____ c. steer

_____ Score 3 points for each correct C answer.

_____ Score 2 points for each correct O answer.

_____ **Total Score:** Using Words Precisely

Enter the four total scores in the spaces below, and add them together to find your Reading Comprehension Score. Then record your score on the graph on page 57.

Score	Question Type	Lesson 4
_____	Finding the Main Idea	
_____	Recalling Facts	
_____	Making Inferences	
_____	Using Words Precisely	
_____	**Reading Comprehension Score**	

Author's Approach

Put an X in the box next to the correct answer.

1. The authors use the first sentence of the article to

☐ a. describe the setting for the beginning of the article.

☐ b. compare hang gliding with water skiing.

☐ c. entertain the reader with a joke.

2. What do the authors mean by the statement "These pilots make [hang gliding] look easy"?

☐ a. The pilots work hard to make the sport look easy so onlookers will admire them.

☐ b. The pilots are so skillful that it seems to onlookers as if they aren't working at the sport at all.

☐ c. The pilots are to blame if inexperienced people get hurt because they haven't stressed how difficult hang gliding really is.

3. Which of the following statements from the article best describes "going over the falls"?

☐ a. [Winds] can cause a glider to take a nosedive straight down.

☐ b. These are tight swirls of air that lift sand, dirt, and bits of litter off the ground.

☐ c. Those are strong winds that come rolling in off mountains.

_____ Number of correct answers

Record your personal assessment of your work on the Critical Thinking Chart on page 58.

Summarizing and Paraphrasing

Follow the directions provided for both questions.

1. Complete the following one-sentence summary of the article using the lettered phrases from the phrase bank below. Write the letters on the lines.

> **Phrase Bank**
> a. the joys of hang gliding
> b. a description of the first time anyone hang glided
> c. the dangers of hang gliding

The article "Hang Gliding" begins with _____, goes on to

explain _____, and ends with _____.

2. Reread paragraph 5 in the article. Below, write a summary of the paragraph in no more than 25 words.

_____

_____

_____

Reread your summary and decide whether it covers the important ideas in the paragraph. Next, decide how to shorten the summary to 15 words or less without leaving out any essential information. Write this summary below.

_____

_____

_____

> _____ Number of correct answers
>
> Record your personal assessment of your work on the Critical Thinking Chart on page 58.

Critical Thinking

Put an X in the box next to the correct answer for questions 1, 3, and 4. Follow the directions provided for the other questions.

1. Which of the following statements from the article is an opinion rather than a fact?

   ☐ a. More than one pilot has died while trying to navigate a glider.

   ☐ b. When hang gliding "pilots" take off, they may plunge through the air in a free fall for 10 or 20 feet.

   ☐ c. In fact, once you're in the air, the ride is much more than simply "OK." It is fantastic.

2. Using what you know about flying an airplane and what is told about hang gliding in the article, name three ways hang gliding is similar to and three ways hang gliding is different from flying an airplane. Cite the paragraph number(s) where you found details in the article to support your conclusions.

Similarities

_____

_____

_____

Differences

_____

_____

_____

3. What was the cause of Bob Abbott's fatal hang gliding accident?

☐ a. A dust devil made him lose control of his glider.

☐ b. A strong wind carried him into a storm.

☐ c. He smashed into some nearby trees.

4. Of the following theme categories, which would this story fit into?

☐ a. Sometimes great inventions happen by accident.

☐ b. If at first you don't succeed, try again.

☐ c. Be careful what you ask for; you might get it.

5. In which paragraph did you find the information or details to answer question 3? _____

_____ Number of correct answers

Record your personal assessment of your work on the Critical Thinking Chart on page 58.

Personal Response

If I were the authors, I would change _____

because _____

_____

_____

_____

Self-Assessment

The part I found most difficult about the article was _____

_____

I found this difficult because _____

_____

_____

_____

Climbing the World's Highest Mountains

Death is everywhere in these mountains. It lurks behind every gust of wind. It hides under every crack in the snow. Dozens of people have died here in the mountains of Asia. Yet climbers keep coming back. They come from around the world to take on peaks such as K2 and Everest.

Climbing a steep slope is hard enough at sea level. But 5½ miles up, it's much harder. The air is thin, the wind is biting, and deep snow hides dangers. In addition, hardy mountain climbers must carry heavy loads. But for some, this is the only way to live.

2   Climbing small mountains is hard enough. You need strong ropes, special boots, and lots of courage. But climbing the world's highest mountains is even tougher. The higher you go, the thinner the air gets. By the time you reach 20,000 feet, your body can hardly function. There is barely enough oxygen in the air to keep you alive.

3   Most climbers carry small tanks of oxygen. But these tanks don't hold much. So parts of the climb must be done on your own. As your brain becomes starved for oxygen, you may find yourself getting dizzy and confused. Your nose might start to bleed. You might feel sick to your stomach. This altitude sickness is no joke. In 1993 a climber on K2 died from it.

4   Others, too, have struggled in the thin air. One was Andrzej Zawada. Zawada was a well-known climber. He had worked his way up many tall mountains. In 1980 he led a group up Mount Everest. At 29,028 feet, it is the highest peak in the world. The climb was a success. But it wasn't easy. "I felt the lack of oxygen very much," Zawada wrote.

5   Zawada's group also had to deal with bad weather. That is a classic problem on these mountains. Temperatures often drop far below zero. Zawada's men were hit by bitterly cold air. At one point, it was 40 degrees below zero *inside their tent!*

6   Sometimes things warm up a bit. Even so, blizzards can move in quickly. K2, the world's second highest mountain, is famous for its storms. They can last for days. They can bury climbers in several feet of new snow. In 1986, five people died when they were trapped in this kind of storm on K2.

7   Each snowfall brings yet another hazard. The weight of new snow can cause an avalanche. If you're caught in an avalanche on Everest or one of the other big mountains, there's not much you can do. Just the thought of being caught in an avalanche makes climbers shiver with fear.

8   Scott Fischer almost died that way. In 1992 he and Ed Viesturs were climbing K2. Suddenly, huge chunks of snow crashed down on them. Fischer was swept down the mountain. Viesturs, who was roped to him, also began to fall. Luckily, Viesturs managed to dig his ice ax into the ground. The two men came to a stop at the edge of a 4,000-foot cliff.

9   Winds also pose a threat. They may whip past at 100 miles per hour. In 1995 Alison Hargreaves fell victim to these winds. Hargreaves was one of the best climbers in the world. She was the first woman ever to reach the top of Mount Everest alone and without an oxygen tank. Only one other person had ever done this before.

10   On August 13, 1995, Hargreaves was on K2. Winds were high. Late that day, she and five other climbers struggled to the top of the mountain. They started back down again. But the winds grew worse, slowing the group's progress. All night, fierce gusts swirled around the mountain. Hargreaves and the others kept going. They tried to get back to their campsite. But they never made it. It appears that sometime during this frightful night, they were swept off their feet. They were literally blown to their deaths. Hargreaves's body was later found in an icy nook not far from camp.

11 And then there is the danger of falling into a crevasse. A crevasse is a narrow crack in the ice. It may be hundreds of feet deep. If there is a little fresh snow covering it, you may not see it until it's too late. Scott Fischer once fell into a crevasse. He didn't fall far, but his body became jammed in the crack. He was locked between two walls of ice. When another climber pulled him out, Fischer found that his right arm had been twisted out of its socket.

12 The list of dangers goes on and on. Mountain climbers can be blinded by the glare of sunlight reflecting off the snow. That happened to Peggy Luce. The year was 1988. Luce was trying to become the second American woman ever to reach the top of Mount Everest. Her goggles became foggy on the way up. She took them off and kept climbing. Luce made it to the top. But as she came back down, she had trouble seeing. She realized she was suffering from snow blindness. People usually recover from this, but it takes a while. Luce knew she had to keep going. She had to get out of the sun and rest her eyes. She stumbled on down the mountain. At one point, she bent over to see where she was putting her foot. She lost her balance. She began to roll down the mountain. Luckily, she dug her ice ax into the snow, stopping her fall. Luce made it to safety. But the next day, her eyes were swollen shut.

13 Sometimes climbers simply run out of energy. Then they might collapse in the snow and wait for death to come. Perhaps that's what happened to a German woman who died on Everest in the 1970s. She was later found, frozen in a sitting position with her head on her knees. "She made it to the top, but she didn't get down," concluded climber David Breashears.

14 Given all the hardships, why do people choose this sport? What makes them run such terrible risks? Many climbers have tried to explain it. Andrzej Zawada said he wanted to "conquer" the highest peaks. Roger Mear said that to succeed when "chances are limited—that's what mountaineering is all about." Giusto Gervasutti called mountain climbing "an inner need." He said it showed "the freedom of the [human] spirit." But perhaps Alison Hargreaves explained it best. Hargreaves knew that someday she might die on a mountain. But as she put it, "One day as a tiger is better than a thousand as a sheep."

If you have been timed while reading this article, enter your reading time below. Then turn to the Words-per-Minute table on page 55 and look up your reading speed (words per minute). Enter your reading speed on the graph on page 56.

Reading Time: Lesson 5

———— : ————
Minutes   Seconds

A | Finding the Main Idea

One statement below expresses the main idea of the article. One statement is too general, or too broad. The other statement explains only part of the article; it is too narrow. Label the statements using the following key:

M—Main Idea   **B—Too Broad**   **N—Too Narrow**

_____ 1. Falling into a crevasse is only one of the many dangers that people face in climbing high mountains.

_____ 2. Climbing very high mountains presents physical problems and dangers more intense than those found in regular mountain climbing.

_____ 3. Climbing mountains takes extraordinary skill, strength, and mental toughness.

_____ Score 15 points for a correct M answer.

_____ Score 5 points for each correct B or N answer.

_____ **Total Score:** Finding the Main Idea

B | Recalling Facts

How well do you remember the facts in the article? Put an X in the box next to the answer that correctly completes each statement about the article.

1. The signs of altitude sickness include
   ☐ a. dizziness, a bloody nose, and vomiting.
   ☐ b. severe headaches.
   ☐ c. inability to see well and loss of memory.

2. Fischer and Viesturs, swept away by an avalanche, were saved when
   ☐ a. a helicopter rescued them.
   ☐ b. their ropes stopped their fall.
   ☐ c. Viesturs dug his ice ax into the ground and stopped their fall.

3. Crevasses are particularly hard to spot because
   ☐ a. they are so deep.
   ☐ b. they are often covered by fresh snow.
   ☐ c. the sunlight reflects off them confusingly.

4. Peggy Luce was the second American woman to
   ☐ a. climb to the top of K2.
   ☐ b. reach the top of Mount Whitney.
   ☐ c. reach the top of Mount Everest.

5. Snow blindness is caused by
   ☐ a. very heavy snowstorms.
   ☐ b. the glare of sunlight reflecting off the snow.
   ☐ c. strong winds blowing the snow around.

Score 5 points for each correct answer.

_____ **Total Score:** Recalling Facts

C | Making Inferences

When you combine your own experience and information from a text to draw a conclusion that is not directly stated in that text, you are making an inference. Below are five statements that may or may not be inferences based on information in the article. Label the statements using the following key:

C—Correct Inference   **F—Faulty Inference**

_____ 1. Climbers who tackle very high mountains should have strong and healthy lungs.

_____ 2. Most people need plenty of oxygen to think clearly.

_____ 3. After you reach the top of a mountain, you can be sure that the worst of the dangers are over.

_____ 4. Winds at the top of a mountain are often stronger than they are in the valley below it.

_____ 5. The best way to climb a high mountain is to go by yourself so you can travel quickly.

Score 5 points for each correct answer.

_____ **Total Score:** Making Inferences

D | Using Words Precisely

Each numbered sentence below contains an underlined word or phrase from the article. Following the sentence are three definitions. One definition is closest to the meaning of the underlined word. One definition is opposite or nearly opposite. Label those two definitions using the following key; do not label the remaining definition.

C—Closest   **O—Opposite or Nearly Opposite**

1. As your brain becomes starved for oxygen, you may find yourself getting dizzy and confused.

_____ a. filled with

_____ b. extremely hungry for

_____ c. aware of

2. This altitude sickness is no joke.

_____ a. depth

_____ b. climbing

_____ c. height

3. That is a classic problem on these mountains.

_____ a. typical

_____ b. dangerous

_____ c. unusual

4. Winds also pose a threat.

_____ a. protection

_____ b. fear

_____ c. danger

5. All night, <u>fierce</u> gusts swirled around the mountain.

_____ a. violent

_____ b. mild

_____ c. cold

_____ Score 3 points for each correct C answer.

_____ Score 2 points for each correct O answer.

_____ **Total Score:** Using Words Precisely

Enter the four total scores in the spaces below, and add them together to find your Reading Comprehension Score. Then record your score on the graph on page 57.

Score	Question Type	Lesson 5
_____	Finding the Main Idea	
_____	Recalling Facts	
_____	Making Inferences	
_____	Using Words Precisely	
_____	**Reading Comprehension Score**	

Author's Approach

Put an X in the box next to the correct answer.

1. The authors use the first sentence of the article to

☐ a. introduce the reader to the climbers the story will focus on.

☐ b. create a tense mood.

☐ c. compare Mount Everest and K2.

2. What is the authors' purpose in writing "Climbing the World's Highest Mountains"?

☐ a. To encourage the reader to take up mountain climbing

☐ b. To inform the reader about the dangers and challenges of high mountain climbing

☐ c. To emphasize the similarities between low mountain climbing and high mountain climbing

3. From the statements below, choose those that you believe the authors would agree with.

☐ a. To climb high mountains, you must be in top physical condition.

☐ b. It is foolish to risk your life just to climb a mountain.

☐ c. The dangers of high mountain climbing are far greater than those that come with climbing lower mountains.

4. The authors tell this story mainly by

☐ a. telling different stories about the same topic.

☐ b. comparing different topics.

☐ c. using their imagination and creativity.

_____ Number of correct answers

Record your personal assessment of your work on the Critical Thinking Chart on page 58.

Summarizing and Paraphrasing

Follow the directions provided for question 1. Put an X in the box next to the correct answer for the other questions.

1. Look for the important ideas and events in paragraphs 11 and 12. Summarize those paragraphs in one or two sentences.

_____

_____

_____

2. Choose the sentence that correctly restates the following sentence from the article: "When another climber pulled him out, Fischer found that his right arm had been twisted out of its socket."

   ☐ a. Fischer twisted his right arm out of its socket by pulling another climber to safety.

   ☐ b. When Fischer twisted his right arm out of its socket, he noticed that another climber had pulled him out.

   ☐ c. Fischer was finally pulled out by another climber. That's when he noticed that his right arm had been twisted out of its socket.

3. Read the statement from the article below. Then read the paraphrase of that statement. Choose the reason that best tells why the paraphrase does not say the same thing as the statement.

   Statement: Alison Hargreaves was the first woman ever to reach the top of Mount Everest alone without using an oxygen tank.

   Paraphrase: The first woman to reach the top of Mount Everest alone was Alison Hargreaves.

   ☐ a. Paraphrase says too much.

   ☐ b. Paraphrase doesn't say enough.

   ☐ c. Paraphrase doesn't agree with the statement.

_____ Number of correct answers

Record your personal assessment of your work on the Critical Thinking Chart on page 58.

Critical Thinking

Put an X in the box next to the correct answer for questions 1, 2, 3, and 4. Follow the directions provided for question 5.

1. Which of the following statements from the article is an opinion rather than a fact?

   ☐ a. Mountain climbers can be blinded by the glare of sunlight reflecting off the snow.

   ☐ b. At 29,028 feet, [Mount Everest] is the highest peak in the world.

   ☐ c. "One day as a tiger is better than a thousand as a sheep."

2. Considering Peggy Luce's actions as told in this article, you can predict that she will

☐ a. never again remove her goggles when climbing on a sunny day.

☐ b. take her goggles off only if she is already on the way down the mountain.

☐ c. wear goggles all the time whenever she climbs mountains, even at night.

3. What is an effect of reduced oxygen in high mountain air?

☐ a. Climbers feel more energy than they do at lower altitudes.

☐ b. Climbers may feel dizzy or sick.

☐ c. Climbers get extremely hungry.

4. How is climbing the highest mountains an example of an extreme sport?

☐ a. To climb the highest mountains, you must be both careful and brave.

☐ b. Climbing the highest mountains is a dangerous sport.

☐ c. To climb the highest mountains, you must push yourself to your physical and mental limits.

5. In which paragraph did you find your information or details to answer question 3? _____

_____ Number of correct answers

Record your personal assessment of your work on the Critical Thinking Chart on page 58.

Personal Response

Begin the first 5–8 sentences of your own article about climbing one of the world's highest mountains. You may tell of a real experience or one that is imagined.

_____

_____

_____

_____

_____

_____

_____

Self-Assessment

A word or phrase in the article that I do not understand is _____

_____

_____

_____

_____

Compare and Contrast

Think about the articles you have read in Unit One. Pick the three sports that you would be most likely to try someday. Write the titles of the articles that tell about them in the first column of the chart below. Use information you learned from the articles to fill in the empty boxes in the chart.

Title	What skills or personal qualities does this sport require?	What are the dangers of the sport?	How could you best train for this sport?

The extreme sport that I would most like to try someday is _____. I chose this sport because

_____

_____

Words-per-Minute Table

Unit One

Directions: If you were timed while reading an article, refer to the Reading Time you recorded in the box at the end of the article. Use this words-per-minute table to determine your reading speed for that article. Then plot your reading speed on the graph on page 56.

Lesson No. of Words	Sample 630	1 1,102	2 894	3 970	4 1073	5 1039	Seconds
1:30	420	735	596	647	715	693	90
1:40	378	661	536	582	644	623	100
1:50	344	601	488	529	585	567	110
2:00	315	551	447	485	537	520	120
2:10	291	509	413	448	495	480	130
2:20	270	472	383	416	460	445	140
2:30	252	441	358	388	429	416	150
2:40	236	412	335	364	402	390	160
2:50	222	389	316	342	379	367	170
3:00	210	367	298	323	358	346	180
3:10	199	348	282	306	339	328	190
3:20	189	331	268	291	322	312	200
3:30	180	315	255	277	307	297	210
3:40	172	301	244	265	293	283	220
3:50	164	287	233	253	280	271	230
4:00	158	276	224	243	268	260	240
4:10	151	264	215	233	258	249	250
4:20	145	254	206	224	248	240	260
4:30	140	245	199	216	238	231	270
4:40	135	236	192	208	230	223	280
4:50	130	228	185	201	222	215	290
5:00	126	220	179	194	215	208	300
5:10	122	213	173	188	208	201	310
5:20	118	207	168	182	201	195	320
5:30	115	200	163	176	195	189	330
5:40	111	194	158	171	189	183	340
5:50	108	189	153	166	184	178	350
6:00	105	184	149	162	179	173	360
6:10	102	179	145	157	174	168	370
6:20	99	174	141	153	169	164	380
6:30	97	170	138	149	165	160	390
6:40	95	165	134	146	161	156	400
6:50	92	161	131	142	157	152	410
7:00	90	157	128	139	153	148	420
7:10	88	154	125	135	150	145	430
7:20	86	150	122	132	146	142	440
7:30	84	147	119	129	143	139	450
7:40	82	144	117	127	140	136	460
7:50	80	141	114	124	137	133	470
8:00	79	138	112	121	134	130	480

Minutes and Seconds

Plotting Your Progress: Reading Speed

Unit One

Directions: If you were timed while reading an article, write your words-per-minute rate for that article in the box under the number of the lesson. Then plot your reading speed on the graph by putting a small X on the line directly above the number of the lesson, across from the number of words per minute you read. As you mark your speed for each lesson, graph your progress by drawing a line to connect the X's.

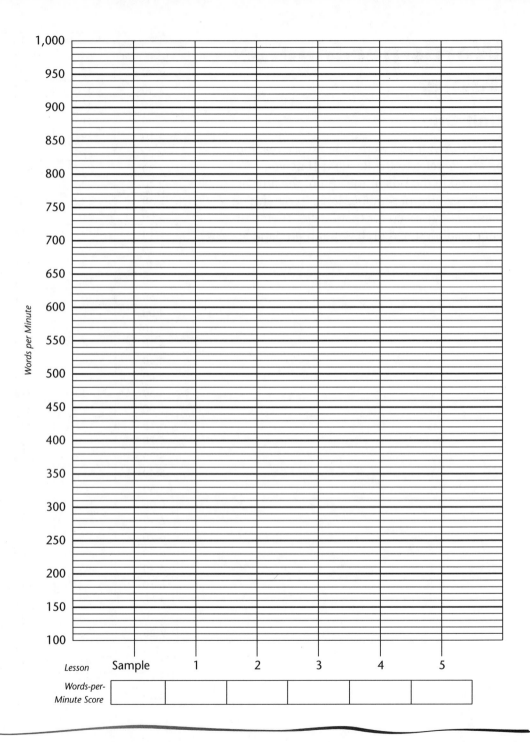

Lesson	Sample	1	2	3	4	5
Words-per-Minute Score						

Plotting Your Progress: Reading Comprehension

Unit One

Directions: Write your Reading Comprehension Score for each lesson in the box under the number of the lesson. Then plot your score on the graph by putting a small X on the line directly above the number of the lesson and across from the score you earned. As you mark your score for each lesson, graph your progress by drawing a line to connect the X's.

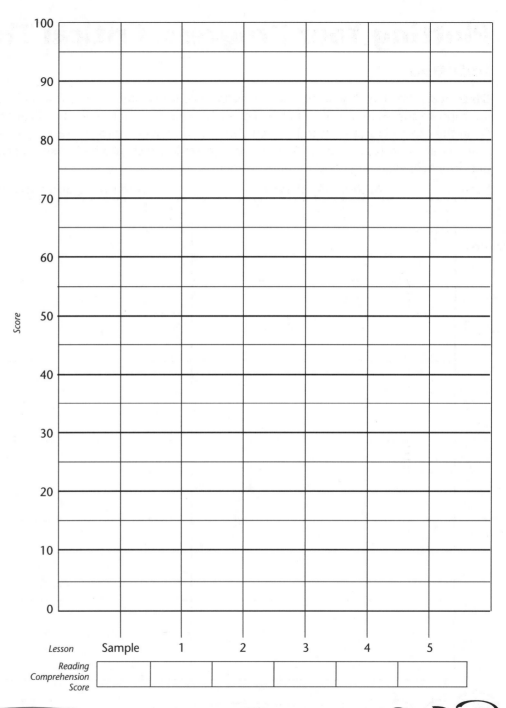

Plotting Your Progress: Critical Thinking

Unit One

Directions: Work with your teacher to evaluate your responses to the Critical Thinking questions for each lesson. Then fill in the appropriate spaces in the chart below. For each lesson and each type of Critical Thinking question, do the following: Mark a minus sign (–) in the box to indicate areas in which you feel you could improve. Mark a plus sign (+) to indicate areas in which you feel you did well. Mark a minus-slash-plus sign (–/+) to indicate areas in which you had mixed success. Then write any comments you have about your performance, including ideas for improvement.

Lesson	Author's Approach	Summarizing and Paraphrasing	Critical Thinking
Sample			
1			
2			
3			
4			
5			

UNIT TWO

The World's Wildest Horse Race

There is no other race in the world like it. It is older than the Kentucky Derby. It is wilder than a three-ring circus. And it is more colorful than halftime at the Super Bowl.

2   The race is the Palio. It is held twice each year in Siena, Italy. The Palio is a horse race with a history going back more than 700 years. It pits the city's 17 districts, or *contrade,* against each other. Each *contrada* has its own flag and its own symbol: the Goose, Wolf, Ram, Snail, and so on. And the rivalries are bitter. "The Palio a serious matter,"

The Palio is a horse race unlike any other. For more than 700 years, fans have been flocking to this wild, no-holds-barred competition that pits 10 districts of Siena, Italy, against each other. When the honor of the contrada is at stake, anything goes!

said one man who lives in Siena. "It's the very life of our contrada."

3   Neighborhood pride runs deep for the people of Siena. Loyalty to one's contrada affects all parts of life. Take, for instance, a woman who—for whatever reason—is about to give birth outside her contrada. Pots of dirt from her district will be rushed to her. These will then be used to support the four legs of her bed. In this way the new baby will be born on home soil. The baby will be baptized twice—once into the church and once into the contrada. When a son marries, it will be in the contrada church. And when he dies, his body will be wrapped in the flag of the contrada.

4   So this is no ordinary race. Some money is bet on the race, but pride is really what's at stake. Everyone wants his or her contrada to win. But winning the Palio isn't easy. First, only 10 horses can run in the race. That means that seven contrade are not even in the event. The ten lucky ones who do race are chosen by lot. Second, the contrade don't get to pick their own horses. Those, too, are chosen by lot. So the horse that won the Palio

last year may be racing for a different contrada this year.

5   Once the horses are assigned, the real fun begins. Each contrada treats its horse like a king. As one man said, "The animal is everything in the Palio." The horse is pampered in every way possible. No one takes any chances with the animal's health. In fact, each horse is guarded day and night. Why? Well, although it's illegal to drug a horse, such tricks have been tried in the past. On the day of the race, each horse is taken to the church of its contrada. There it is blessed and sprinkled with holy water.

6   The jockeys who ride these horses are professionals. They come from all over Italy. Each contrada hires the best jockey it can find. The jockeys are in the race just for the money. So they will work for whatever contrada makes them the best offer. That contrada is not always the one that hired them in the first place. You see, the Palio is the most corrupt horse race in the world. In the United States it is illegal to fix a horse race. In Siena it's a tradition!

7   The people of one contrada often try to bribe other jockeys to lose the race on purpose. To prevent that, each contrada hires a guard to watch its rider. But then the guard might be bribed. So each contrada has to hire a second guard to watch over the first one. This scheming goes on right up until the start of the race.

8   On the day of the race, there is a huge parade. Marchers from each contrada parade through the city streets. Flag bearers lead the way. They are followed by young men dressed in wigs and medieval clothes. Then comes the jockey, dressed as a knight in shining armor. He is followed by a boy leading the contrada's racehorse. At last, the parade ends. Each knight casts off his armor and hops onto his horse. The race is about to begin.

9   The Palio is held in the heart of the city on July 2 and August 16. The horses race around the edge of a brick-paved square called the Piazza del Campo. The course is dangerous. It contains two sharp turns and lies on the pitch of a hillside. The horses must go around the course three times to win. The winner is the first horse to cross the finish line—with or without a jockey! The prize is the Palio, a silk banner bearing the image of the Virgin Mary.

10   The race itself is a wild affair. The jockeys must ride bareback. They wear steel helmets for protection. The horses line up behind a rope. The starter drops a match onto some loose gunpowder. BOOM! The rope drops and the horses and jockeys leap into action. At this point, anything goes. The jockeys can—and do—whip each other. They may slam each other into walls, many of which are covered with mattresses to avoid serious injuries. Sometimes horses and jockeys are knocked to the ground. A fallen jockey might then stand on the track and try to knock down other jockeys.

11   Meanwhile, the 70,000 fans jammed into the piazza go wild. People faint from all the excitement. Dozens of fights break out in the stands. When the race ends, citizens from the winning contrada cheer loudly. They rush to hug the jockey and caress the horse. They then march through the streets of the city, boasting and taunting. The winning contrada will party all through the night. The losers can't wait for the next Palio—and revenge.

If you have been timed while reading this article, enter your reading time below. Then turn to the Words-per-Minute table on page 101 and look up your reading speed (words per minute). Enter your reading speed on the graph on page 102.

Reading Time: Lesson 6

—————— : ——————
Minutes   Seconds

A Finding the Main Idea

One statement below expresses the main idea of the article. One statement is too general, or too broad. The other statement explains only part of the article; it is too narrow. Label the statements using the following key:

M—Main Idea   B—Too Broad   N—Too Narrow

_____ 1. Horse racing has been one of the world's most popular sports for hundreds of years, and the Palio of Siena, Italy, is one of the oldest horse races.

_____ 2. The Palio of Siena, Italy, a horse race held twice a year, is a good-natured rivalry where the only rule is that almost anything goes.

_____ 3. On the day of the Palio, a famous horse race of Siena, each horse is taken to its contrada's church to be blessed and sprinkled with holy water.

_____ Score 15 points for a correct M answer.

_____ Score 5 points for each correct B or N answer.

_____ **Total Score:** Finding the Main Idea

B Recalling Facts

How well do you remember the facts in the article? Put an X in the box next to the answer that correctly completes each statement about the article.

1. The contrade that compete in the Palio are the
   - [ ] a. most important families of Siena.
   - [ ] b. town's major business interests.
   - [ ] c. ancient districts of the city.

2. Horses are assigned to run for the various contrade
   - [ ] a. by a lottery.
   - [ ] b. by a complicated scheduling system.
   - [ ] c. through bribery.

3. People in Siena expect every jockey to
   - [ ] a. train hard for this event.
   - [ ] b. accept bribes from several contrade.
   - [ ] c. remain loyal to one contrada for life.

4. The race is held
   - [ ] a. on a racecourse just outside of town.
   - [ ] b. on a racecourse within the city walls.
   - [ ] c. in the Piazza del Campo.

5. In order to win, a horse must
   - [ ] a. circle the piazza three times and reach the finish line first, with or without its jockey.
   - [ ] b. carry its rider, wearing full armor, to the finish line.
   - [ ] c. try to bump into other horses during the race.

Score 5 points for each correct answer.

_____ **Total Score:** Recalling Facts

63

C Making Inferences

When you combine your own experience and information from a text to draw a conclusion that is not directly stated in that text, you are making an inference. Below are five statements that may or may not be inferences based on information in the article. Label the statements using the following key:

C—Correct Inference   **F—Faulty Inference**

_____ 1. Most natives of Siena's contrade frequently move from one district of the city to another.

_____ 2. Citizens of a contrada trust their horse to do its best much more than they trust the contrada's jockey to do so.

_____ 3. The people of Siena would agree that moving the race to a new, state-of-the-art racecourse would make the Palio even more exciting.

_____ 4. Jockeys may make more money when they lose the Palio than when they win.

_____ 5. Only tourists interested in the Palio should take rooms next to the Piazza del Campo for the dates of the race.

Score 5 points for each correct answer.

_____ **Total Score:** Making Inferences

D Using Words Precisely

Each numbered sentence below contains an underlined word or phrase from the article. Following the sentence are three definitions. One definition is closest to the meaning of the underlined word. One definition is opposite or nearly opposite. Label those two definitions using the following key; do not label the remaining definition.

C—Closest   **O—Opposite or Nearly Opposite**

1. <u>Loyalty</u> to one's contrada affects all parts of life.

_____ a. closeness

_____ b. betrayal

_____ c. faithfulness

2. Once the horses are <u>assigned</u>, the real fun begins.

_____ a. given out

_____ b. taken back

_____ c. set aside

3. The horse is <u>pampered</u> in every way possible.

_____ a. trained

_____ b. spoiled

_____ c. punished

4. You see, the Palio is the most <u>corrupt</u> horse race in the world.

_____ a. dishonest

_____ b. pure

_____ c. dangerous

5. The course is dangerous. It contains two sharp turns and lies on the <u>pitch</u> of the hillside.

_____ a. rise

_____ b. slope

_____ c. value

_____ Score 3 points for each correct C answer.

_____ Score 2 points for each correct O answer.

_____ **Total Score:** Using Words Precisely

Enter the four total scores in the spaces below, and add them together to find your Reading Comprehension Score. Then record your score on the graph on page 103.

Score	Question Type	Lesson 6
_____	Finding the Main Idea	
_____	Recalling Facts	
_____	Making Inferences	
_____	Using Words Precisely	
_____	**Reading Comprehension Score**	

Author's Approach

Put an X in the box next to the correct answer.

1. What do the authors mean by the statement "In the United States it is illegal to fix a horse race"?

☐ a. In the United States, racing horses is illegal.

☐ b. In the United States, it is against the law to improve a horse race.

☐ c. In the United States, it is against the law to arrange the winner of a horse race before it begins.

2. The main purpose of the first paragraph is to

☐ a. inform the reader about how the Palio began.

☐ b. describe the qualities of the Palio.

☐ c. explain the rules of the Palio.

3. What is the authors' purpose in writing "The World's Wildest Horse Race"?

☐ a. to encourage the reader to plan a race like the Palio

☐ b. to inform the reader about a unique and exciting horse race

☐ c. to describe a situation in which people use dirty tricks to succeed

4. In this article, "The 10 lucky [contrade] who do race are chosen by lot" means

☐ a. the contrade who are allowed to race are chosen by chance, as in a drawing.

☐ b. lots of contrade are allowed to race.

☐ c. a lot of people choose the contrade who are allowed to race.

_____ Number of correct answers

Record your personal assessment of your work on the Critical Thinking Chart on page 104.

Summarizing and Paraphrasing

Put an X in the box next to the correct answer for questions 1 and 3. Follow the directions provided for question 2.

1. Below are summaries of the article. Choose the summary that says all the most important things about the article but in the fewest words.

   ☐ a. Horses in the Palio race around the Piazza del Campo in Siena, Italy. The winning contrada is presented with a silk banner bearing the image of the Virgin Mary.

   ☐ b. The Palio horse race in Siena, Italy, is a wild, no-holds-barred affair held twice a year in the heart of the city. Sections of the city, called contrade, compete against each other to win the race, and no dirty trick is illegal.

   ☐ c. People of Siena, Italy, take the Palio very seriously. Local pride is at stake when the horses run the race twice each year, on July 2 and August 16.

2. Reread paragraph 4 in the article. Below, write a summary of the paragraph in no more than 25 words.

   _____

   _____

   _____

   _____

   Reread your summary and decide whether it covers the important ideas in the paragraph. Next, decide how to shorten the summary to 15 words or less without leaving out any essential information. Write this summary below.

   _____

   _____

   _____

3. Choose the best one-sentence paraphrase for the following sentence from the article: "[The jockeys] may slam each other into walls, many of which are covered with mattresses to avoid serious injuries."

   ☐ a. Jockeys may push each other into walls that are covered with mattresses. The mattresses prevent the jockeys from being seriously injured.

   ☐ b. Jockeys covered with mattresses slam each other into walls to avoid injuries.

   ☐ c. To avoid injuries, jockeys slam each other into walls covered with mattresses.

   _____ Number of correct answers

   Record your personal assessment of your work on the Critical Thinking Chart on page 104.

Critical Thinking

Follow the directions provided for questions 1, 3, 4, and 5. Put an X in the box next to the correct answer for question 2.

1. For each statement below, write *O* if it expresses an opinion or write *F* if it expresses a fact.

   _____ a. The Palio began about 700 years ago.

   _____ b. Anyone who visits Siena, Italy, for the Palio will have a wonderful time.

   _____ c. The Palio is disgraceful because it encourages cheating.

2. From what the article told about how the race is run, you can predict that

☐ a. jockeys sometimes get hurt.

☐ b. horses never escape the race unharmed.

☐ c. no fan has ever been injured during the race.

3. Choose from the letters below to correctly complete the following statement. Write the letters on the lines.

On the positive side, _____, but on the negative side, _____.

  a. the race is held twice a year

  b. people may get hurt during the race

  c. the people of Siena enjoy the competition

4. Think about cause-effect relationships in the article. Fill in the blanks in the cause-effect chart, drawing from the letters below.

Cause	Effect
Mothers want their children born on home soil.	_____
Sometimes other contrade try to bribe the jockey.	_____
Walls are covered with soft mattresses.	_____

  a. Jockeys are not hurt when they push each other into walls during the race.

  b. People set the bed of a woman giving birth on pots of dirt from her district.

  c. A guard watches the jockey at all times.

5. Which paragraphs from the article provide evidence that supports your answer to question 4? _____

_____ Number of correct answers

Record your personal assessment of your work on the Critical Thinking Chart on page 104.

Personal Response

This article is different from other articles about extreme sports I've read because _____

and Palio is unlike other races because _____

_____

_____

_____

Self-Assessment

I was confused on question _____ in the _____

section because _____

_____

_____

_____

Skiing the Impossible

Is Kristen Ulmer out of her mind? You might think so when she describes some of the jumps she's made on skis. For instance, there was the time she flew through the air so out of control that she fainted from fear. Luckily, she didn't kill herself. But she did crash into a tree. Still, Ulmer didn't quit skiing. Instead, she went out looking for even bigger jumps.

2   Ulmer is one of a small band of extreme skiers who feel they have outgrown normal skiing. Normal ski

No, this skier did not take a wrong turn and wind up in the wrong place. She MEANT to ski off this cliff! She has taken up the most dangerous form of skiing, called extreme skiing.

trails are marked. Signs tell everyone how hard the different trails are. Green circles are easy paths for "snow bunnies." Blue squares are harder, but they can be skied by most good skiers. Black diamonds are steep trails for experts only. Black diamonds offer plenty of excitement for most people. But not for Kristen Ulmer and friends. To them, all marked trails look too tame. They want to ski the impossible!

3   What qualifies as "impossible"? You can take your pick. Some extreme skiers love to ski off cliffs. A man named Terry Cook does backflips off 60-foot cliffs. Others like to ski in the narrow openings between cliffs. Scott Schmidt is known for skiing along thin strips of snow that cut through the mountains of Italy. He zips through passageways with huge walls of rock on either side. Sometimes the passageways are no more than 10 feet wide. One slip and he'll smash into the rocks. "It's like skiing through a twisted cave," Schmidt says. "The light is dim and far above you, and the rock walls blur as you rocket past."

4   Others enjoy the thrill of skiing down a glacier in Antarctica. Some, meanwhile, choose to ski the summits of huge mountains in Asia. You get the point: extreme skiers live to prove that what seems impossible really can be done.

5   Once a slope has been conquered, extreme skiers often move on to something else. The idea is to find a place that no one has ever skied before. Scott Schmidt does that. As he climbs up cliffs, he is always searching for "something tougher." As Schmidt says, "I [spend] all that energy hauling my skis up there, and I [don't] want to waste it just repeating the old stuff."

6   Pierre Tardivel, a top extreme skier from France, feels the same way. "I'm not interested if something *has* been done," he says. "I want to know if it *can* be done. That's the adventure."

7   Tardivel has skied nearly 50 "firsts." He was the first to ski the south summit of Mount Everest. At 28,766 feet, that's higher than anyone on skis had ever been. Tardivel is an expert at skiing down steep terrain. Most black diamond trails have slopes no steeper than 30 degrees. Tardivel skis slopes of 45 to 60 degrees! Imagine standing up straight on such a steep slope. At 45 degrees you could reach out and touch the snow with your hand. At 60 degrees you could touch it with your elbow!

8   Tardivel takes his time when he skis a new place. He doesn't simply tuck and race down. That would be suicide. Instead, he picks his way along, making one or two turns at a time. He has to plan every move. That way he can avoid ice and boulders that often litter the run. Even so, he usually slides 50 feet or more before the edges of his skis grab enough to stop.

9   People can die skiing the "impossible." Tardivel knows that better than most. And he says he doesn't want to die. There is a saying in extreme sports: "live and learn; learn or die." So Tardivel always climbs up a new run before he skis down it. When asked why, he answers, "Gouvy and Moroni."

10   Bruno Gouvy and Alain Moroni were extreme skiers. Both died because they didn't climb up a new run before they skied down it. Gouvy took a helicopter to the summit of a mountain in France. He didn't know there was black ice beneath the snow. He slipped and fell to his death.

Moroni rode a ski lift to a summit and walked over to a new place he wanted to try. He, too, fell to his death. "Both were killed because they started from the top," says Tardivel.

11 Why do extreme skiers risk their lives in the first place? To most of us, it seems they must have a death wish. But they deny that. They say it isn't a matter of courting death. It's a matter of facing your fears and overcoming them. That's why Scott Schmidt became interested in the sport. As a child, Schmidt liked to be pulled along behind his father's snowmobile. One day his father tried to take him over a "monster two-foot jump." Recalls Scott, "I chickened out and let go of the rope right on the lip. That's when I started confronting my fears." The best way to do that, he found, was by extreme skiing.

12 Conquering your fear is not the same as losing your fear. In fact, extreme skiers say the fear is always there. "You've got to have some fear of what you're doing or else you don't belong out there," declares extreme skier Dean Cummings.

13 "We all know extreme skiing is dangerous," echoes Kristen Ulmer. But she insists it's worth the risks. For her, it's about "the need to be the best you can be and to express that through what you do." Also, Ulmer says, extreme skiing helps you believe in yourself. You become your own superhero. You learn to have complete faith in your abilities. That faith, she says, "is absolutely essential if you want to be an extreme skier."

14 Extreme skiers now compete against each other. Every year they face off in the World Extreme Skiing Championship. This event is not open to everyone. You have to be well prepared. You have to prove that you have skied at least four extreme descents. Skiers must be expert mountain climbers. And they must be trained in avoiding and surviving avalanches.

15 In the championship, the skiers are taken to the top of some wild peak. As they ski down, judges grade them on style and difficulty. If you win—great. But just staying alive is also a triumph. In 1993 a skier died when the snow ledge he was on gave way. For safety,

skiers must wear avalanche beacons. That makes it possible for rescuers to locate them and try to save them.

16 Dean Cummings once barely escaped death. He was caught in an avalanche and almost tumbled over a 100-foot cliff. What did he think about his brush with death? It was a contest between sheer fright and wild fun. And fun won. Cummings calls his experience "the most incredible buzz you could ever have." It's thoughts like this that make Ulmer, Tardivel, and Cummings "extreme." The rest of us can find plenty of "buzz" on regular ski trails.

A Finding the Main Idea

One statement below expresses the main idea of the article. One statement is too general, or too broad. The other statement explains only part of the article; it is too narrow. Label the statements using the following key:

M—Main Idea   **B—Too Broad**   **N—Too Narrow**

_____ 1. Extreme skiing, that is, skiing in areas that are usually considered impossible to ski, is a sport that requires strength and daring.

_____ 2. People who like excitement and the chance to test their own personal limits would enjoy extreme skiing.

_____ 3. Extreme skier Pierre Tardivel was the first to ski the south summit of Mount Everest.

_____ Score 15 points for a correct M answer.

_____ Score 5 points for each correct B or N answer.

_____ **Total Score:** Finding the Main Idea

B Recalling Facts

How well do you remember the facts in the article? Put an X in the box next to the answer that correctly completes each statement about the article.

1. A black diamond on a trail marker means that the trail is
   - ☐ a. easy enough for beginners.
   - ☐ b. possible for most good skiers.
   - ☐ c. full of steep places for expert skiers only.

2. Extreme skier Pierre Tardivel always climbs a new run before he skis down it, because he
   - ☐ a. enjoys mountain climbing as much as skiing.
   - ☐ b. wants to learn about its hazards.
   - ☐ c. is afraid of ski lifts.

3. A slope of 45 degrees would be
   - ☐ a. easy to ski.
   - ☐ b. good for an expert skier.
   - ☐ c. fit only for an extreme skier to try.

4. Judges grade extreme skiers on their
   - ☐ a. style and the difficulty of the descent.
   - ☐ b. speed in coming down the mountain.
   - ☐ c. attention to safety rules.

5. Skiers wear avalanche beacons because beacons
   - ☐ a. make it easier for the judges to see them.
   - ☐ b. will help rescuers locate them.
   - ☐ c. can keep the skiers warm.

Score 5 points for each correct answer.

_____ **Total Score:** Recalling Facts

C Making Inferences

When you combine your own experience and information from a text to draw a conclusion that is not directly stated in that text, you are making an inference. Below are five statements that may or may not be inferences based on information in the article. Label the statements using the following key:

C—Correct Inference **F—Faulty Inference**

_____ 1. Most of the time, extreme skiers would welcome a group of inexperienced skiers to join them on their mountain runs.

_____ 2. Skier Pierre Tardivel has climbed the south summit of Mount Everest.

_____ 3. If extreme skiers didn't ski, they probably would find another way to test their strength and courage.

_____ 4. A person with little self-confidence would be most likely to take up extreme skiing.

_____ 5. The organizers of the World Extreme Skiing Championship are concerned about the safety of the skiers.

Score 5 points for each correct answer.

_____ **Total Score:** Making Inferences

D Using Words Precisely

Each numbered sentence below contains an underlined word or phrase from the article. Following the sentence are three definitions. One definition is closest to the meaning of the underlined word. One definition is opposite or nearly opposite. Label those two definitions using the following key; do not label the remaining definition.

C—Closest **O—Opposite or Nearly Opposite**

1. That way he can avoid ice and boulders that often <u>litter</u> the run.

_____ a. make clean and orderly

_____ b. build

_____ c. clutter up

2. Moroni rode a ski lift to a <u>summit</u> and walked over to a new place he wanted to try.

_____ a. hotel

_____ b. peak

_____ c. base

3. They say it isn't a matter of <u>courting</u> death.

_____ a. looking for

_____ b. trying to avoid

_____ c. understanding

4. He doesn't simply <u>tuck</u> and race down.

_____ a. crouch

_____ b. look carefully

_____ c. stretch out

5. But just staying alive is also a <u>triumph</u>.

_____ a. surprise

_____ b. defeat

_____ c. victory

Enter the four total scores in the spaces below, and add them together to find your Reading Comprehension Score. Then record your score on the graph on page 103.

Author's Approach

Put an X in the box next to the correct answer.

1. What is the authors' purpose in writing "Skiing the Impossible"?

☐ a. to make the reader embarrassed to do regular skiing

☐ b. to inform the reader about what extreme skiers do and why they do it

☐ c. to emphasize the differences between skiing and snowboarding

2. Which two of the following statements from the article best describe good places to do impossible skiing?

☐ a. Green circles are easy paths for "snow bunnies."

☐ b. He zips through passageways with huge walls of rock on either side. Sometimes the passageways are no more than 10 feet wide.

☐ c. He was the first to ski the south summit of Mount Everest.

3. Choose the statement below that is the weakest argument for extreme skiing.

☐ a. Extreme skiing is never boring.

☐ b. By doing extreme skiing, you can conquer your fears and begin to trust yourself.

☐ c. Extreme skiing can kill you.

4. The authors tell this story mainly by

☐ a. comparing different topics.

☐ b. using his or her imagination and creativity.

☐ c. telling different stories about the same topic.

Summarizing and Paraphrasing

Follow the directions provided for question 1. Put an X in the box next to the correct answer for question 2.

1. Reread paragraph 8 in the article. Below, write a summary of the paragraph in no more than 25 words.

_____

_____

_____

_____

Reread your summary and decide whether it covers the important ideas in the paragraph. Next, decide how to shorten the summary to 15 words or less without leaving out any essential information. Write this summary below.

_____

_____

_____

2. Read the statement about the article below. Then read the paraphrase of that statement. Choose the reason that best tells why the paraphrase does not say the same thing as the statement.

Statement: Participants at the annual World Extreme Skiing Championship must be both experienced extreme skiers and expert mountain climbers.

Paraphrase: Only experienced extreme skiers may participate in the annual World Extreme Skiing Championship.

☐ a. Paraphrase says too much.

☐ b. Paraphrase doesn't say enough.

☐ c. Paraphrase doesn't agree with the statement.

_____ Number of correct answers

Record your personal assessment of your work on the Critical Thinking Chart on page 104.

Critical Thinking

Follow the directions provided for questions 1, 2, 3, and 5.
Put an X in the box next to the correct answer for question 4.

1. For each statement below, write *O* if it expresses an opinion or write *F* if it expresses a fact.

_____ a. Extreme skiers are braver than any other athletes.

_____ b. Especially steep ski trails are marked with black diamonds.

_____ c. Extreme skiers usually check out their routes thoroughly before starting down.

2. Choose from the letters below to correctly complete the following statement. Write the letters on the lines.

In the article, _____ and _____ are different.

a. the difficulty of skiing where Pierre Tardivel skis

b. the difficulty of skiing where a regular skier skis

c. the difficulty of skiing where Kristen Ulmer skis

3. Choose from the letters below to correctly complete the following statement. Write the letters on the lines.

According to the article, _____ caused Bruno Gouvy to _____, and the effect was _____.

a. overlook the fact that there was black ice under the snow

b. Gouvy slipped and fell to his death

c. taking a helicopter to the summit of a mountain

4. How is "Skiing the Impossible" an example of an extreme sport?

☐ a. The skiers are seeking ways to prove themselves with feats few others can do.

☐ b. It takes skill and courage.

☐ c. The skiers are often frightened before they start down, but they overcome their fears.

5. In which paragraph did you find your information or details to answer question 3? _____

_____ Number of correct answers

Record your personal assessment of your work on the Critical Thinking Chart on page 104.

Personal Response

I can't believe _____

_____

_____

Self-Assessment

One good question about this article that was not asked would be

_____

_____

And the answer is _____

_____

_____

Race Through the Sand

So you like to run? You really, *really* like to run? Then maybe the Marathon of the Sands is for you. Of course, you'll have to fly to Morocco to take part in it. You'll have to run 140 miles in seven days. And you'll have to do it all in 120° F heat.

2   Clearly the Marathon of the Sands is no ordinary race. Organizers boast that it is "the world's toughest footrace." It consists of six stages, each one stretching out across the brutally hot Sahara desert. Runners don't just have to carry themselves across the sand.

A normal 26-mile marathon? That's for weaklings. Extreme athletes compete in ultramarathons, in which runners cover 50, 100, or even 500 miles. The Marathon of the Sands features the added attractions of extreme heat and assorted desert hazards.

They have to carry all their food and equipment, too. That means running with a backpack full of freeze-dried meals, sleeping bag, clothes, compass, distress flare—and, oh yes, a snakebite kit.

3   Each year, about 500 people sign up to run this grueling race, known to many by its French name, *Marathon des Sables*. The race began in 1986. Since then, only one runner has died. The victim was a Frenchman in his 20s. He died of a heart attack in the blistering heat. But while most people don't die, they do suffer. Over the years, dozens have dropped out from dehydration or heat exhaustion. Some have collapsed with sunstroke. And even those who have finished wind up in plenty of pain. One doctor described it this way. "The blisters on top of blisters, sunburn, windburn . . . sore, aching muscles, swollen feet . . . puffy faces, sunken eyelids, peeling and flaking skin. . . ."

4   The day before the race, runners are told what the course will be. It varies each year. But always it winds through the Moroccan Sahara. That means it cuts across some of the hottest land on

earth. At night, the temperature may dip to 40°F. But in the daytime it often stays around 120°F. Runners' feet swell so much that they need shoes two sizes larger than normal. Everyone puts on lots of sunscreen. Even so, runners end up with skin that is red and blistered.

5   Race officials provide all runners with nine liters of water each day. That is not much in the desert heat. If runners get too dehydrated, they can get fluids through an intravenous feeding. But those who get two of these IVs are out of the race. So most runners stagger on even as thirst racks their bodies.

6   Besides the intense sun and heat, there is always the threat of a sandstorm. One sandstorm swept through the desert during the 1996 race. "The sand hit me like thousands of tiny needles," one man said. "Sand crept into every crevice of my clothing and body. I felt like I was wrapped in sandpaper."

7   Sometimes runners become lost in the endless dunes. In 1994 an Italian runner took a wrong turn. He spent the next nine days wandering through

the desert. During that time he lost more than 30 pounds. He survived only by drinking his own urine and the blood of dead bats.

8 In 1997 runner Cathy Tibbetts found out that even the sand beneath her feet could be a hazard. Tibbetts was running in shoes with mesh tops. She thought they would help keep her feet cool. But the mesh let all the sand in. "Fine grains poured through the mesh," she said. "I had to stop and empty my shoes so often it cost me hours of time."

9 When the runners aren't kicking their way through sand, they are running over hard rocks. "Most people envision the Sahara Desert as nothing but dunes," Tibbetts says. "But in reality there are more rocks than sand." Runners who trip on these rocks end up with cuts, bruises, and fractured bones.

10 At night runners face new problems. They have to make their meager rations last all week. Often they go to bed hungry. Lying in their communal tents, they have to hope that no scorpions crawl into their bedrolls.

11 The longest stage of the race is a 47-mile run. It comes on Day 4 of the race. This stage brings even top

athletes to their knees. Runners vomit. They pass out. They cry. Yet most of them keep going.

12 Why do people put themselves through such torture? Well, they don't do it for the money. It costs close to $3,000 to participate in the Marathon of the Sands. First prize is only $5,000.

13 The runners themselves joke about their reasons. "Behind the sand dunes, you can meet wonderful girls," quipped one. Another said he entered "because I am mad." In truth, though, these runners like the challenge. They like to test themselves. A good way to do that is to run long distances in tough surroundings. Mary Gadams has run in many ultramarathons. "Yet no event has captivated me more than the Marathon des Sables," she says.

14 Runner Maurice Daubard put it this way. "Suffering is everywhere. It is the human condition. Yet suffering has much to teach."

15 Perhaps that's what Frenchman Patrick Bauer was thinking when he set up this race. In 1984 Bauer walked 200 miles through the Algerian part of the Sahara. After he finished, he wanted to share the experience with

others. And so he started the Marathon of the Sands.

16 Runners have to get their doctors' permission to join the race. Beyond that, almost anyone can run. Runners have been as young as 16 and as old as 76. They have come from all around the world. In 2000 they came from about 30 countries.

17 So if you want to make a really long run, think about the Marathon of the Sands. And don't be puzzled by the $250 "corpse repatriation fee." That money will be used to fly your body home if you don't survive!

A | Finding the Main Idea

One statement below expresses the main idea of the article. One statement is too general, or too broad. The other statement explains only part of the article; it is too narrow. Label the statements using the following key:

M—Main Idea   **B—Too Broad**   **N—Too Narrow**

_____ 1. Many athletes love the challenge of competitions that demand extraordinary strength, courage, and perseverance.

_____ 2. Runners from all over the world participate in the tough Marathon of the Sands, which leads them 140 miles across the Sahara Desert in 120° F heat.

_____ 3. Runners in the grueling Marathon of the Sands often drop out because of dehydration, heat exhaustion, or sunstroke.

_____ Score 15 points for a correct M answer.

_____ Score 5 points for each correct B or N answer.

_____ **Total Score:** Finding the Main Idea

B | Recalling Facts

How well do you remember the facts in the article? Put an X in the box next to the answer that correctly completes each statement about the article.

1. The Marathon of the Sands is run in the
   - ☐ a. Gobi Desert.
   - ☐ b. Sahara Desert.
   - ☐ c. Mojave Desert.

2. In the desert the daytime temperature can reach a high of
   - ☐ a. 120°F.
   - ☐ b. 40°F.
   - ☐ c. 85°F.

3. The abbreviation *IV* stands for
   - ☐ a. "intervention."
   - ☐ b. "international venue."
   - ☐ c. "intravenous feeding."

4. The race's most difficult stage is the
   - ☐ a. 47-mile run.
   - ☐ b. 140-mile run.
   - ☐ c. 99-mile run.

5. The winner of the race is awarded
   - ☐ a. a trophy.
   - ☐ b. $5,000.
   - ☐ c. one million dollars.

Score 5 points for each correct answer.

_____ **Total Score:** Recalling Facts

C Making Inferences

When you combine your own experience with information from a text to draw a conclusion that is not directly stated in that text, you are making an inference. Below are five statements that may or may not be inferences based on information in the article. Label the statements using the following key:

C—Correct Inference   **F—Faulty Inference**

_____ 1. The race course for Marathon of the Sands is clearly marked with temporary signs.

_____ 2. Medical help for the runners is available occasionally.

_____ 3. The prize given to the winner of the race will make him or her wealthy for life.

_____ 4. Many of the runners who compete in this race are in poor physical condition even before they begin.

_____ 5. Not even the strongest sunscreen can protect a person from sunburn if he or she is out in the desert all day.

Score 5 points for each correct answer.

_____ **Total Score:** Making Inferences

D Using Words Precisely

Each numbered sentence below contains an underlined word or phrase from the article. Following the sentence are three definitions. One definition is closest to the meaning of the underlined word. One definition is opposite or nearly opposite. Label those two definitions using the following key; do not label the remaining definition.

C—Closest   **O—Opposite or Nearly Opposite**

1. If runners get too <u>dehydrated</u>, they can get fluids through an intravenous feeding.

_____ a. tired

_____ b. dried out

_____ c. wet

2. "Yet no event has <u>captivated</u> me more than the Marathon des Sables," she says.

_____ a. fascinated

_____ b. puzzled

_____ c. bored

3. They have to make their <u>meager</u> rations last all week.

_____ a. generous

_____ b. delicious

_____ c. skimpy

4. Lying in their <u>communal</u> tents, they have to hope that no scorpions crawl into their bedrolls.

_____ a. shared

_____ b. separate

_____ c. uncomfortable

5. "Behind the sand dunes, you can meet wonderful girls," quipped one.

_____ a. said in a serious manner

_____ b. heard

_____ c. joked

_____ Score 3 points for each correct C answer.

_____ Score 2 points for each correct O answer.

_____ **Total Score:** Using Words Precisely

Enter the four total scores in the spaces below, and add them together to find your Reading Comprehension Score. Then record your score on the graph on page 103.

Score	Question Type	Lesson 8
_____	Finding the Main Idea	
_____	Recalling Facts	
_____	Making Inferences	
_____	Using Words Precisely	
_____	**Reading Comprehension Score**	

Author's Approach

Put an X in the box next to the correct answer.

1. The main purpose of the first paragraph is to
   - ☐ a. summarize requirements of the Marathon of the Sands.
   - ☐ b. entertain the reader with a joke.
   - ☐ c. persuade the reader to become a marathon runner.

2. What is the authors' purpose in writing "Race Through the Sand"?
   - ☐ a. to express an opinion about marathon running
   - ☐ b. to inform the reader about weather conditions in the desert
   - ☐ c. to describe a situation in which people risk their health to prove their courage

3. Which of the following statements from the article best describes runners at night on the desert?
   - ☐ a. Runners vomit. They pass out. They cry.
   - ☐ b. Some have collapsed with sunstroke.
   - ☐ c. Lying in their communal tents, they have to hope that no scorpions crawl into their bedrolls.

4. What do the authors imply by saying "Sometimes runners become lost in the endless dunes"?
   - ☐ a. Runners never have any way of knowing where they are.
   - ☐ b. Runners do not all run together, as a group.
   - ☐ c. Runners are not given instructions about where to run.

_____ Number of correct answers

Record your personal assessment of your work on the Critical Thinking Chart on page 104.

Summarizing and Paraphrasing

Put an X in the box next to the correct answer for questions 1 and 3. Follow the directions provided for question 2.

1. Below are summaries of the article. Choose the summary that says all the most important things about the article but in the fewest words.

    ☐ a. The Marathon of the Sands is a race that was set up by a man who wanted to share the experience of traveling on foot through the desert. The 140-mile race takes several days and demands that runners withstand heat, sun, exhaustion, and pain.

    ☐ b. Although the prize for winning the Marathon of the Sands is only $5,000, people from all over the world have participated in it. In 2000, for example, runners came from about 30 countries.

    ☐ c. Wearing the proper shoes in a race such as the Marathon of the Sands can mean the difference between winning and losing. Runner Cathy Tibbetts wore shoes made of mesh and found that she had to stop often to empty sand out of her shoes.

2. Reread paragraph 9 in the article. Below, write a summary of the paragraph in no more than 25 words.

    _____

    _____

    _____

    _____

Reread your summary and decide whether it covers the important ideas in the paragraph. Next, decide how to shorten the summary to 15 words or less without leaving out any essential information. Write this summary below.

_____

_____

_____

3. Choose the best one-sentence paraphrase for the following sentence from the article: "This stage brings even top athletes to their knees."

    ☐ a. Top athletes often stumble and fall when they reach this stage.

    ☐ b. Even top athletes have difficulty at this stage.

    ☐ c. The knees of even the best athletes give them trouble at this stage.

_____ Number of correct answers

Record your personal assessment of your work on the Critical Thinking Chart on page 104.

CRITICAL THINKING

Critical Thinking

Put an X in the box next to the correct answer for the following questions.

1. From what Cathy Tibbetts said, you can predict that the next time she runs in the Marathon of the Sands, she will

☐ a. advertise and sell her mesh shoes to other runners.

☐ b. wear the mesh shoes again.

☐ c. wear a pair of shoes not made of mesh.

2. What is the effect on a runner of having officials to give him or her two intravenous feedings?

☐ a. The runner is out of the race.

☐ b. The runner is placed ahead of the other runners.

☐ c. The runner gets a private tent at the next stop.

3. Why is the Marathon of the Sands considered an extreme sport?

☐ a. Because the race is in the desert, runners are hot during the day and cold at night.

☐ b. The race could end in injury or even death for runners who are not incredibly fit and lucky.

☐ c. Runners participate because they enjoy the challenge.

4. What did you have to do to answer question 1?

☐ a. find an opinion (what someone thinks about something)

☐ b. make a prediction (what will happen next)

☐ c. find a cause (why something happened)

_____ Number of correct answers

Record your personal assessment of your work on the Critical Thinking Chart on page 104.

Personal Response

What new question do you have about this topic?

_____

_____

_____

_____

Self-Assessment

A word or phrase in the article that I do not understand is _____

_____

_____

_____

Stunt Flying

Charles Hamilton was no fool. "We shall all be killed if we stay in the business," he said. Hamilton was lucky. He ended up dying a natural death. But many of his friends died in balls of flames. What "business" was Hamilton in? He was a stunt flier. He and other daredevil pilots enthralled fans with their high-risk moves in the sky.

2   It all began around 1910. Aviation was new. Many people were thrilled just to see a plane. And when that

During the 1920s, fans were thrilled by the sight of daring stunt pilots who put on "flying circuses." Ormer Locklear was a famous stunt flyer who appeared in air shows all around the country in the decade following World War I.

plane started doing tricks—well, it was better than a trip to the circus. In fact that was what stunt pilots called their acts: flying circuses.

3   One of the first great stunt pilots was Lincoln Beachey. He could do amazing things in the flimsy planes of the day. He could, for instance, pick a handkerchief off the airfield with his wing tip. In 1911 Beachey stunned people when he flew *under* the bridge at Niagara Falls. But his boldest stunt was to fly straight up until he ran out of gas. Then, somehow, he glided his "dead" plane safely back to earth.

4   In 1912 Beachey got a call from Glenn Curtiss. Curtiss made airplanes. He wanted to sell his planes to the U.S. Army. But the Army was not convinced that Curtiss planes could do a tight figure eight. Curtiss wanted to show the Army what his product could really do. So he asked Beachey to fly a demonstration. Beachey flew a tighter figure eight than anyone had ever seen. The next day, Army officials asked Beachey for a favor. They asked him never to fly on an Army airfield

again! The reason? They worried that their own pilots would try to copy Beachey's stunt and get killed.

5   Instead, it was Beachey who got killed. It happened in 1915. He was doing an air show in California. During a difficult trick, the wings on his plane broke. More than 50,000 fans watched in horror as Beachey's plane spun out of control and crashed.

6   Still, people kept coming back for more. Air shows really took off after World War I ended in 1918. The Army had trained lots of pilots. Suddenly, these men had nothing to do. Many bought their own planes and became stunt fliers. Planes were cheap in those days—about $600 apiece. And with the war over, there were plenty of planes for sale.

7   The most popular model was a double-winged plane called a Jenny. It was designed to carry two people. Pilots said this plane could land on a dime. They flew their Jennies from town to town, putting on air shows. They used open farm fields for landing and taking off. At night, they put their airplanes into nearby barns for shelter. These men, plus a few equally bold

women pilots, became known as "barnstormers."

8   People flocked to see the air shows. Many of the stunts were truly death defying. Pilots flew upside down. They did loops close to the ground. Sometimes a pilot took along a partner who jumped out of the plane in the middle of the show. To fans who didn't know what a parachute was, this move came as a real shock!

9   As the years went by, air shows grew more and more outrageous. Pilots began working with "wing walkers." These people did all sorts of crazy things on the wings of planes. Gladys Roy wowed people by dancing the Charleston on the upper wing. Mabel Cody often "fell" off a wing. She would save herself by grabbing a cord hanging from the airplane. Then, she would place the cord between her teeth and begin to spin around. People always gasped when they saw this Iron Jaw Spin.

10   Duke Krantz amazed crowds by hanging from a wing by his toes. One day Krantz really stunned his fans. He climbed to the top wing. Then the pilot went into a steep dive and ended in a full loop. All this

time, Krantz remained standing on the wing. A hidden cable held him in place. But for a few moments, the awestruck crowd felt sure he would plunge to his death.

11   The fact that some pilots *did* fall to their deaths added to the thrill. Laura Bromwell fell out of her cockpit during a loop. She was more than 1,000 feet in the air at the time. She did not survive the fall.

12   Sometimes two pilots would team up. With two planes in the air, wing walkers could really go wild. Ethel Dare, known as the Flying Witch, had a daring trick. She would climb down a rope ladder from one plane, then jump to the wing of a second plane. That act was later banned, however, when a man was killed trying to perform it.

13   By 1930 air shows were dying out. New laws against low-level flying forced many shows to close. Besides, flying was now seen as serious business. Pilots took on new challenges. Charles Lindbergh started out as a barnstormer, but in 1924 he became an army pilot. Three years later, he made the first solo, nonstop

flight across the Atlantic Ocean. Clyde "Upside-Down" Pangborn spent years in a flying circus. Then he turned to long-distance flight. In 1931 he made the first nonstop trip across the Pacific.

14   Still, the attraction of stunt flying never completely died. In recent years, air shows have been on the rise again. Now most shows feature jets, not Jennies. But the element of danger remains. In 1988 German pilots held a big air show. Pilots in nine jets traced a big heart across the sky. A tenth pilot tried to draw a line of smoke straight through the figure. It was supposed to be an arrow piercing the heart. But this tenth jet didn't move fast enough. It hit one of the other planes, causing them both to crash into the crowd. Forty-nine people died.

15   Lee Oman had a close call in a 1991 air show. Oman liked to perform a trick on an old-fashioned, double-winged plane. He hung from a bar below the plane. He moved his legs as though walking in midair. One day, though, his hands slipped off the bar. He fell 10 feet before the harness he was wearing

caught him. He dangled helplessly from the harness, having no way to get back up to the bar. The pilot had to drop him onto a speeding truck in order to save his life.

16   In 1991 Joann Osterud found a way to combine stunt flying and long-distance flying. She set a new record for the longest flight made upside-down. She flew her biplane that way for four hours and 38 minutes. She covered 658 miles. Clearly, in Osterud, Oman, and others like them, the tradition of stunt flying is alive and well.

If you have been timed while reading this article, enter your reading time below. Then turn to the Words-per-Minute table on page 101 and look up your reading speed (words per minute). Enter your reading speed on the graph on page 102.

Reading Time: Lesson 9

————— : —————
Minutes   Seconds

A | Finding the Main Idea

One statement below expresses the main idea of the article. One statement is too general, or too broad. The other statement explains only part of the article; it is too narrow. Label the statements using the following key:

M—Main Idea   **B—Too Broad**   **N—Too Narrow**

_____ 1. Since the beginnings of aviation around 1910, stunt fliers have created thrills with their daring piloting, wing walking, and other moves on planes.

_____ 2. The invention of the airplane at the beginning of the 20th century opened the skies to adventurous men and women.

_____ 3. Charles Lindbergh, who started his career as a barnstormer, gained fame in 1927 when he made the first solo, nonstop flight across the Atlantic Ocean.

_____ Score 15 points for a correct M answer.

_____ Score 5 points for each correct B or N answer.

_____ **Total Score:** Finding the Main Idea

B | Recalling Facts

How well do you remember the facts in the article? Put an X in the box next to the answer that correctly completes each statement about the article.

1. Lincoln Beachey proved to the U.S. Army that
   □ a. a person could walk on a plane wing.
   □ b. a Curtiss plane could fly a tight figure eight.
   □ c. planes could be used reliably in warfare.

2. After World War I, a small plane cost about
   □ a. $60.
   □ b. $600.
   □ c. $6,000.

3. Mabel Cody pretended to fall off a wing, saved herself by grabbing a cord, and then
   □ a. climbed the cord back up to the wing.
   □ b. dropped to earth with a parachute.
   □ c. put the cord between her teeth and spun.

4. Clyde Pangborn was the first person to fly
   □ a. nonstop from Maine to California.
   □ b. solo across the Atlantic.
   □ c. nonstop across the Pacific.

5. In 1991 Joann Osterud set a new record for the longest
   □ a. flight made upside-down.
   □ b. time spent wing walking.
   □ c. flight in a World War I plane.

Score 5 points for each correct answer.

_____ **Total Score:** Recalling Facts

87

C Making Inferences

When you combine your own experience and information from a text to draw a conclusion that is not directly stated in that text, you are making an inference. Below are five statements that may or may not be inferences based on information in the article. Label the statements using the following key:

C—Correct Inference   **F—Faulty Inference**

_____ 1. In the early days of flying, there were few laws limiting what could be done with planes.

_____ 2. The planes called Jennies required a long and very level runway for taking off and landing.

_____ 3. Many early planes did not have seatbelts.

_____ 4. Lincoln Beachey would have been happy to become a test pilot.

_____ 5. As people become more familiar with planes, they will lose all interest in the stunt flying of today and yesterday.

Score 5 points for each correct answer.

_____ **Total Score:** Making Inferences

D Using Words Precisely

Each numbered sentence below contains an underlined word or phrase from the article. Following the sentence are three definitions. One definition is closest to the meaning of the underlined word. One definition is opposite or nearly opposite. Label those two definitions using the following key; do not label the remaining definition.

C—Closest   **O—Opposite or Nearly Opposite**

1. He and other daredevil pilots <u>enthralled</u> fans with their high-risk moves in the sky.

_____ a. repelled; drove away

_____ b. fascinated

_____ c. changed the opinions of

2. He could do amazing things in the <u>flimsy</u> planes of the day.

_____ a. fragile; easily broken

_____ b. small; hard to see

_____ c. strong; well-built

3. Many of the stunts were truly death <u>defying</u>.

_____ a. organizing

_____ b. challenging

_____ c. obeying

4. Gladys Roy <u>wowed</u> people by dancing the Charleston on the upper wing.

_____ a. paid

_____ b. bored

_____ c. dazzled

5. A hidden cable held him in place. But for a few moments, the <u>awestruck</u> crowd felt sure he would plunge to his death.

_____ a. scornful

_____ b. noisy

_____ c. amazed

_____ Score 3 points for each correct C answer.

_____ Score 2 points for each correct O answer.

_____ **Total Score:** Using Words Precisely

Enter the four total scores in the spaces below, and add them together to find your Reading Comprehension Score. Then record your score on the graph on page 103.

Score	Question Type	Lesson 9
_____	Finding the Main Idea	
_____	Recalling Facts	
_____	Making Inferences	
_____	Using Words Precisely	
_____	**Reading Comprehension Score**	

Author's Approach

Put an X in the box next to the correct answer.

1. The main purpose of the first paragraph is to

☐ a. compare stunt flying and regular flying.

☐ b. make the reader feel sorry for stunt fliers.

☐ c. emphasize the risk involved in stunt flying.

2. From the statements below, choose those that you believe the authors would agree with.

☐ a. Stunt fliers are willing to take enormous risks.

☐ b. Stunt pilots have amazing control over their planes.

☐ c. Planes are too expensive today.

3. In this article, "Pilots said this plane could land on a dime" means

☐ a. pilots claimed that the plane was easy to maneuver and could land in a small space.

☐ b. pilots reported that the plane was quite safe.

☐ c. pilots claimed that this plane was comfortable and efficient.

4. Choose the statement below that best describes the authors' position in paragraph 16.

☐ a. Joann Osterud set a record for the longest flight made upside-down.

☐ b. Stunt flying is still a popular sport.

☐ c. Stunt flying can be successfully combined with long-distance flying.

_____ Number of correct answers

Record your personal assessment of your work on the Critical Thinking Chart on page 104.

Summarizing and Paraphrasing

Follow the directions provided for questions 1 and 2. Put an X in the box next to the correct answer for question 3.

1. Look for the important ideas and events in paragraphs 3 and 4. Summarize those paragraphs in one or two sentences.

_____

_____

_____

2. Complete the following one-sentence summary of the article using the lettered phrases from the phrase bank below. Write the letters on the lines.

> ### Phrase Bank
> a. modern stunt fliers
> b. the acts that stunt fliers were famous for
> c. explaining how stunt flying began

The article "Stunt Flying" begins by _____, goes on to describe _____, and ends by talking about _____.

3. Read the statement about the article below. Then read the paraphrase of that statement. Choose the reason that best tells why the paraphrase does not say the same thing as the statement.

Statement: One stunt pilot who died during her act was Laura Bromwell, who fell more than 1,000 feet.

Paraphrase: Stunt pilot Laura Bromwell fell out of her plane during a loop and tumbled more than 1,000 feet to her death.

☐ a. Paraphrase says too much.

☐ b. Paraphrase doesn't say enough.

☐ c. Paraphrase doesn't agree with the statement.

> _____ Number of correct answers
>
> Record your personal assessment of your work on the Critical Thinking Chart on page 104.

Critical Thinking

Put an X in the box next to the correct answer for questions 1 and 4. Follow the directions provided for the other questions.

1. Which of the following statements from the article is an opinion rather than a fact?

☐ a. Sometimes a pilot took along a partner who jumped out of the plane in the middle of the show.

☐ b. New laws against low-level flying forced many shows to close.

☐ c. And when that plane started doing tricks—well, it was better than a trip to the circus.

2. Choose from the letters below to correctly complete the following statement. Write the letters on the lines.

In the article, _____ and _____ are alike.

a. the popularity of stunt flying in the 1920s

b. the popularity of stunt flying in the 1930s

c. the popularity of stunt flying today

3. Reread paragraph 13. Then choose from the letters below to correctly complete the following statement. Write the letters on the lines.

According to paragraph 13, _____ happened because _____.

a. the government passed new laws against low-level flying

b. the closing of many air shows

c. Charles Lindbergh's career as a barnstormer

4. What did you have to do to answer question 2?

☐ a. find an opinion (what someone thinks about something)

☐ b. find a description (how something looks)

☐ c. find a comparison (how things are the same)

_____ Number of correct answers

Record your personal assessment of your work on the Critical Thinking Chart on page 104.

Personal Response

What was most surprising or interesting to you about this article?

_____

_____

_____

Self-Assessment

Which concepts or ideas from the article were difficult to understand?

_____

_____

_____

Which were easy?

_____

_____

_____

CRITICAL THINKING

The Last Great Race on Earth

In 1925 a diphtheria epidemic threatened Nome, Alaska. Medicine had to be carried from Nenana to Nome to save the town. A relay of several dog teams transported the precious serum 674 miles in less than five days. Today the Iditarod commemorates that incredible journey.

Iditarod racers can be tall or short, young or old, men or women. There's only one thing they cannot be: cowards. If they are, they will never survive this grueling 1,160-mile race.

2   In the Iditarod, each racer travels alone on a sled pulled by dogs. The idea is to get from one end of Alaska to the other as fast as possible. That means all the racers—or *mushers,* as they are called—push themselves and their dogs to the limit. Sometimes dogs die along the way. Mushers know that they, too, might die. Still, every year people return to run this "Last Great Race on Earth."

3   The race begins in the city of Anchorage. Mushers harness their best 15 or 20 sled dogs. They jump onto sleds packed with food and other supplies. Then they head out. The race course follows an old mail route that used to pass through Alaska's mining towns. But since the towns are mostly deserted now, the race is one long trek through the wilderness. Mushers stop at 18 checkpoints along the way. Otherwise, they have no contact with the outside world until they reach the finish line in Nome.

4   With luck, the first hours of the race go smoothly. The dogs find their rhythm. The teams catch every twist and turn in the trail. The mushers can settle back and enjoy the snowy silence of the Alaskan frontier.

5   Sooner or later, though, trouble is bound to arise. The dogs may stumble on rough ground, cutting their paws on razor-sharp slivers of ice. Or the dogs might make a wrong turn. Then a musher may wander miles off the trail. Frozen lakes and rivers can also spell disaster. If the ice is not thick enough, the entire team can fall through, pulling the musher into the icy water. If that happens, there is little chance of getting out alive.

6   Then there are the storms. Four-time Iditarod winner Susan Butcher knows all about storms. She once hit a blizzard that left 30-foot high snowdrifts. In 1985, winner Libby Riddles tried to push her way through a terrible storm. Conditions were so bad that for 11 hours she could not move at all. The first time Gary Paulsen tried the Iditarod, he got stuck in "a killing storm."

7   Paulsen was way out on the trail when the storm hit. He was miles from the nearest checkpoint. "The wind must have been blowing 70 or 80 miles per hour," he later wrote. "I knew it was impossible to do anything but hunker down and try to survive." Paulsen stopped his sled and climbed into his sleeping bag. His dogs lay down in the snow, curling up into tight little balls. Hours later, after the snow finally stopped, Paulsen and the dogs dug themselves out. Then they resumed the race.

8   Even if mushers avoid blizzards, there is no way to avoid the bitter cold. Temperatures on the trail can drop to 50 or 60 degrees below zero.

One musher reported air so cold it froze the batteries in his flashlight. His wooden matches would not light. In weather like that, frostbite sets in quickly. Mushers may arrive at the finish line with frostbitten cheeks, toes, or fingers.

9   Certain parts of the trail hold special dangers. Farewell Burn is a 92 mile stretch of burned-out forest. The winds that whip through there blow all the snow away. So the dogs must pick their way around rocks, blackened stumps, and water holes. One year, Susan Butcher's sled crashed into a tree as she raced through the Burn. Butcher and four of her dogs were hurt in the accident.

10   For some, the toughest part of the trail is Rainy Pass. Here mushers must steer their sleds along a narrow ledge. One wrong move can send them tumbling to their deaths in a rock-filled gorge. For others, Happy River is the worst. To reach it, mushers have to navigate a 500-foot drop into a canyon. Then, after crossing the river, they have to climb out the other side.

11   All of these dangers would be hard enough to face in broad daylight on a good night's sleep. But Iditarod mushers travel at night as well as during the day. And they don't get a good night's sleep. In fact, they don't get much sleep at all. They make many short stops to feed their dogs, but that's not a time for sleeping. At checkpoints, they may take a longer break, but even then, there is a lot to do. Mushers need to check their dogs' paws for cuts. They have to rub their dogs' sore muscles. They may also need to repair their sleds or fix a broken harness. Sometimes mushers grab a few hours' sleep at a checkpoint. But often they stay just a few minutes, then head out again.

12   By the middle of the race, then, lack of sleep becomes a real issue. Many mushers begin to doze on the sled. They have to trust their dogs to keep running in the right direction. Some exhausted mushers begin to hallucinate. They see things that are not there. Some see imaginary trees or lakes. Gary Paulsen saw everything from his wife to a man in a suit to the coast of California!

13   Storms, lack of sleep, and frigid temperatures are always part of the race. But once in a while, mushers run into something more. They come across a crazed moose. Gary Paulsen was run over by such a moose. Luckily, Paulsen was not badly hurt. But that same moose killed a dog in another musher's team.

14   Susan Butcher's team was also attacked by a moose one year. Butcher tried to scare the moose off with an ax. But again and again, the animal tried to trample her dogs. After 20 minutes, musher Dave Halverson happened by. Halverson, who kept a gun in his sled, quickly shot the moose. By then, two of Butcher's dogs were dead and most of the others were injured. So Butcher was forced to drop out of the race.

15   Dropping out of the Iditarod is not cause for shame. When things go wrong, even the best mushers have to call it quits. Still, the thrill of crossing that finish line keeps many of them going. In 1995 Doug Swingley set a new speed record for the race. He completed the course in just nine days, two hours, and 42 minutes. To do that, he averaged much more than a 100 miles a day. But even for mushers who take twice as long to finish, the Iditarod is still the thrill of a lifetime.

If you have been timed while reading this article, enter your reading time below. Then turn to the Words-per-Minute table on page 101 and look up your reading speed (words per minute). Enter your reading speed on the graph on page 102.

Reading Time: Lesson 10

_____ : _____
Minutes   Seconds

A Finding the Main Idea

One statement below expresses the main idea of the article. One statement is too general, or too broad. The other statement explains only part of the article; it is too narrow. Label the statements using the following key:

M—Main Idea   **B—Too Broad**   **N—Too Narrow**

_____ 1. In the Iditarod, exhausted racers often fall asleep or see imaginary things along the trail, and their dogs must move forward without guidance.

_____ 2. Weariness, bad weather, and hazards along the trail make the Iditarod sled race across Alaska a great but dangerous challenge to each racer.

_____ 3. There are few races anywhere in the world more thrilling than the annual Iditarod dogsled race in Alaska.

_____ Score 15 points for a correct M answer.

_____ Score 5 points for each correct B or N answer.

_____ **Total Score:** Finding the Main Idea

B Recalling Facts

How well do you remember the facts in the article? Put an X in the box next to the answer that correctly completes each statement about the article.

1. The Iditarod sled race begins in the city of
   ☐ a. Nome.
   ☐ b. Anchorage.
   ☐ c. Fairbanks.

2. During the race, mushers must stop at
   ☐ a. dusk.
   ☐ b. 15 checkpoints.
   ☐ c. 18 checkpoints.

3. Each team consists of
   ☐ a. one racer and a dozen or more dogs.
   ☐ b. one main racer, his or her alternate, and a dozen or more dogs.
   ☐ c. one racer, a dozen or more dogs, and a support crew that brings in fresh dogs.

4. When Gary Paulsen was caught in a blizzard, he
   ☐ a. waited it out in a deserted mining town.
   ☐ b. lay down in the snow until the storm ended.
   ☐ c. had to quit the race.

5. Once, two of Susan Butcher's dogs were killed
   ☐ a. by a powerful and angry moose.
   ☐ b. when they fell through thin ice on a lake.
   ☐ c. when they lost their footing in a canyon.

Score 5 points for each correct answer.

_____ **Total Score:** Recalling Facts

C Making Inferences

When you combine your own experience and information from a text to draw a conclusion that is not directly stated in that text, you are making an inference. Below are five statements that may or may not be inferences based on information in the article. Label the statements using the following key:

C—Correct Inference   F—Faulty Inference

_____ 1. To have a good chance of winning the Iditarod, mushers and their dogs must be in good physical shape and get along well with each other.

_____ 2. Large areas of Alaska have few, if any, settlers.

_____ 3. Athletes who know how to swim and climb mountains have an advantage as mushers in the Iditarod.

_____ 4. It is unlikely that huge numbers of spectators will ever line the Iditarod course, as they do at the Indy 500 or the Kentucky Derby.

_____ 5. Competition between mushers is so fierce that each one is happy when storms, accidents, or other dangers cause problems for his or her rivals.

Score 5 points for each correct answer.

_____ **Total Score:** Making Inferences

D Using Words Precisely

Each numbered sentence below contains an underlined word or phrase from the article. Following the sentence are three definitions. One definition is closest to the meaning of the underlined word. One definition is opposite or nearly opposite. Label those two definitions using the following key; do not label the remaining definition.

C—Closest   O—Opposite or Nearly Opposite

1. There's only one thing they cannot be: cowards. If they are, they will never survive this grueling 1,160-mile race.

_____ a. popular

_____ b. very difficult

_____ c. easy

2. Hours later, after the snow finally stopped, Paulsen and the dogs dug themselves out. Then they resumed the race.

_____ a. stopped

_____ b. watched

_____ c. began again after an interruption

3. Some exhausted mushers begin to hallucinate.

_____ a. extremely tired

_____ b. fresh; full of energy

_____ c. unfriendly

4. Some exhausted mushers begin to hallucinate.

_____ a. speak loudly

_____ b. face reality

_____ c. have fantasies

5. Butcher tried to scare the moose off with an ax. But again and again, the animal tried to <u>trample</u> her dogs.

_____ a. beat down with one's feet

_____ b. gore

_____ c. lift up

_____ Score 3 points for each correct C answer.

_____ Score 2 points for each correct O answer.

_____ **Total Score:** Using Words Precisely

Enter the four total scores in the spaces below, and add them together to find your Reading Comprehension Score. Then record your score on the graph on page 103.

Score	Question Type	Lesson 10
_____	Finding the Main Idea	
_____	Recalling Facts	
_____	Making Inferences	
_____	Using Words Precisely	
_____	**Reading Comprehension Score**	

Author's Approach

Put an X in the box next to the correct answer.

1. What is the authors' purpose in writing "The Last Great Race on Earth"?

☐ a. to encourage the reader to move to Alaska

☐ b. to inform the reader about weather conditions in Alaska

☐ c. to describe a situation in which athletes face extreme dangers to win a race

2. Which of the following passages from the article best describes a danger faced by Iditarod racers?

☐ a. The dogs find their rhythm. The teams catch every twist and turn in the trail.

☐ b. The race begins in the city of Anchorage. Mushers harness their best 15 or 20 sled dogs.

☐ c. But once in a while, mushers run into something more. They come across a crazed moose.

3. What do the authors imply by saying "After 20 minutes, musher Dave Halverson happened by"?

☐ a. Twenty minutes later, by chance, musher Dave Halverson came on the scene.

☐ b. Musher Dave Halverson was scheduled to stop by and he finally arrived 20 minutes later.

☐ c. Musher Dave Halverson waited too long before he decided to stop by.

_____ Number of correct answers

Record your personal assessment of your work on the Critical Thinking Chart on page 104.

Summarizing and Paraphrasing

Follow the directions provided for questions 1 and 2. Put an X in the box next to the correct answer for question 3.

1. Look for the important ideas and events in paragraphs 10 and 11. Summarize those paragraphs in one or two sentences.

_____

_____

_____

2. Complete the following one-sentence summary of the article using the lettered phrases from the phrase bank below. Write the letters on the lines.

> **Phrase Bank**
> a. a look at people who cross the finish line
> b. the start of the race
> c. the dangers that racers face along the trail

The article "The Last Great Race on Earth" begins with
_____, goes on to explain _____, and ends with
_____.

3. Choose the sentence that correctly restates the following sentence from the article: "If the ice is not thick enough, the entire team can fall through, pulling the musher into the icy water."

☐ a. The thick ice pulled the entire team and the musher into the icy water.

☐ b. The entire team, along with the musher, may fall into icy water if the ice is not thick enough.

☐ c. The musher may fall through the ice, pulling the entire team into the icy water.

_____ Number of correct answers

Record your personal assessment of your work on the Critical Thinking Chart on page 104.

Critical Thinking

Put an X in the box next to the correct answer for questions 1, 3, 4, and 5. Follow the directions provided for question 2.

1. From the article, you can predict that if Dave Halverson had not come by when Susan Butcher's team was attacked by a moose,

☐ a. Susan Butcher would have eventually scared off the moose.

☐ b. all the dogs would have been trampled.

☐ c. the moose would soon have lost interest and left Butcher and her dogs alone.

2. Choose from the letters below to correctly complete the following statement. Write the letters on the lines.

On the positive side, _____, but on the negative side,

_____.

   a. the Iditarod gives racers a chance to test their courage and strength

   b. the record time for finishing the Iditarod is nine days, two hours, and 42 minutes

   c. the Iditarod usually causes suffering for the human and dog participants

3. What is the effect of the racers' lack of sleep by the middle of the race?

☐ a. The racers develop frostbite on their cheeks, toes, and fingers.

☐ b. The racers fall asleep on the sled as they race, and they begin to hallucinate.

☐ c. Racers run into terrible storms.

4. If you were a musher in the Iditarod, how could you use the information in the article to win the race and arrive at the finish line safely?

☐ a. Unlike other mushers, maintain a regular sleep schedule.

☐ b. Refuse to quit the race, no matter what happens to you or to your dogs.

☐ c. Pack lots of supplies and a warm sleeping bag.

5. What did you have to do to answer question 4?

☐ a. find a comparison (how things are the same)

☐ b. find a description (how something looks)

☐ c. draw a conclusion (a sensible statement based on the text and your experience)

_____ Number of correct answers

Record your personal assessment of your work on the Critical Thinking Chart on page 104.

Personal Response

What would you have done if, like Susan Butcher, you encountered a blizzard with 30-foot drifts along the trail?

_____

_____

_____

_____

Self-Assessment

I can't really understand how _____

_____

_____

Compare and Contrast

Think about the articles you have read in Unit Two. Pick the three sports or events that you would most enjoy covering for a TV or radio report. Write the titles of the articles that tell about them in the first column of the chart below. Use information you learned from the articles to fill in the empty boxes in the chart.

Title	Where would you need to go to view this sport or event?	Who participates in this sport?	What parts of this sport would your audience find most interesting?

Imagine that you are reporting on the following sporting event: _____. Write a short speech to introduce your audience to your coverage . _____

_____

_____

Words-per-Minute Table

Unit Two

Directions: If you were timed while reading an article, refer to the Reading Time you recorded in the box at the end of the article. Use this words-per-minute table to determine your reading speed for that article. Then plot your reading speed on the graph on page 102.

Lesson No. of Words	6 921	7 1,154	8 935	9 1,127	10 1097	
1:30	614	763	623	751	731	**90**
1:40	553	692	561	676	658	**100**
1:50	502	629	510	615	598	**110**
2:00	461	577	468	564	549	**120**
2:10	425	533	432	520	506	**130**
2:20	395	495	401	483	470	**140**
2:30	368	462	374	451	439	**150**
2:40	345	433	351	423	411	**160**
2:50	325	407	330	398	387	**170**
3:00	307	385	312	376	366	**180**
3:10	231	364	295	356	346	**190**
3:20	276	346	281	338	329	**200**
3:30	263	330	267	322	313	**210**
3:40	251	315	255	307	299	**220**
3:50	240	301	244	294	286	**230**
4:00	230	289	234	282	274	**240**
4:10	221	277	224	270	263	**250**
4:20	213	266	216	260	253	**260**
4:30	205	256	208	250	244	**270**
4:40	197	247	200	242	235	**280**
4:50	191	239	193	233	227	**290**
5:00	184	231	187	225	219	**300**
5:10	178	223	181	218	212	**310**
5:20	173	216	175	211	206	**320**
5:30	167	210	170	205	199	**330**
5:40	163	204	165	199	194	**340**
5:50	158	198	160	193	188	**350**
6:00	154	192	156	188	183	**360**
6:10	149	187	152	183	178	**370**
6:20	145	182	148	178	173	**380**
6:30	142	178	144	179	169	**390**
6:40	138	173	140	169	165	**400**
6:50	135	169	137	165	161	**410**
7:00	132	165	134	161	157	**420**
7:10	129	161	130	157	153	**430**
7:20	126	157	128	154	150	**440**
7:30	123	154	125	150	146	**450**
7:40	120	151	122	147	143	**460**
7:50	118	147	119	144	140	**470**
8:00	115	144	117	141	137	**480**

Minutes and Seconds

Seconds

Plotting Your Progress: Reading Speed

Unit Two

Directions: If you were timed while reading an article, write your words-per-minute rate for that article in the box under the number of the lesson. Then plot your reading speed on the graph by putting a small X on the line directly above the number of the lesson, across from the number of words per minute you read. As you mark your speed for each lesson, graph your progress by drawing a line to connect the X's.

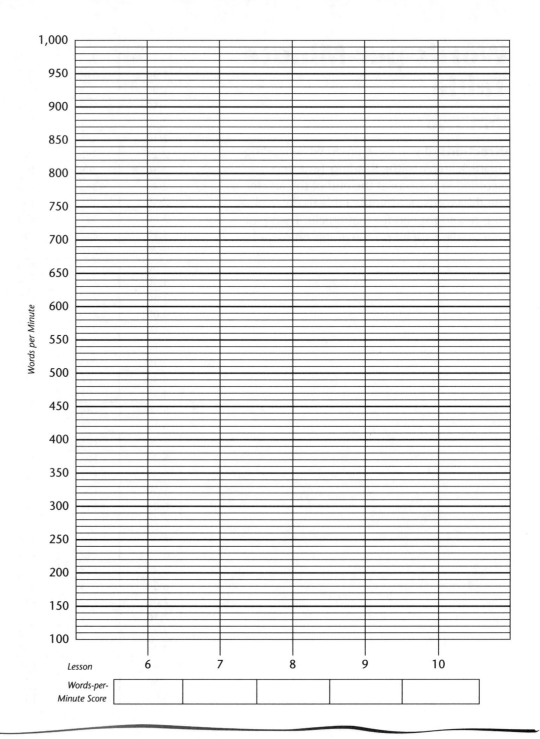

Words per Minute

Lesson	6	7	8	9	10
Words-per-Minute Score					

Plotting Your Progress: Reading Comprehension

Unit Two

Directions: Write your Reading Comprehension Score for each lesson in the box under the number of the lesson. Then plot your score on the graph by putting a small X on the line directly above the number of the lesson and across from the score you earned. As you mark your score for each lesson, graph your progress by drawing a line to connect the X's.

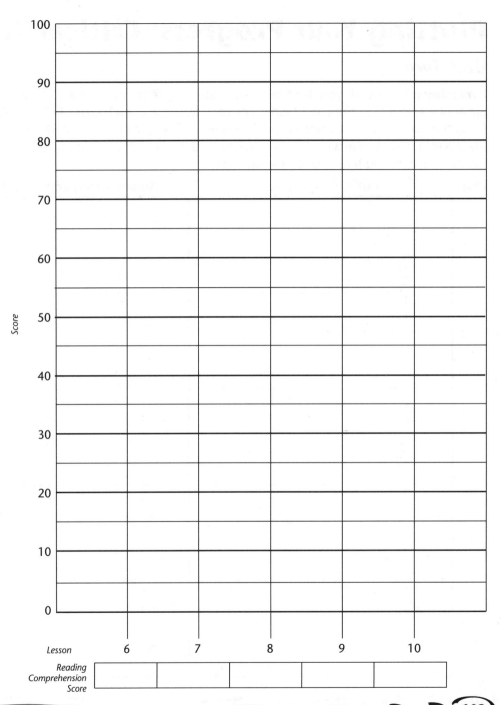

Plotting Your Progress: Critical Thinking

Unit Two

Directions: Work with your teacher to evaluate your responses to the Critical Thinking questions for each lesson. Then fill in the appropriate spaces in the chart below. For each lesson and each type of Critical Thinking question, do the following: Mark a minus sign (–) in the box to indicate areas in which you feel you could improve. Mark a plus sign (+) to indicate areas in which you feel you did well. Mark a minus-slash-plus sign (–/+) to indicate areas in which you had mixed success. Then write any comments you have about your performance, including ideas for improvement.

Lesson	Author's Approach	Summarizing and Paraphrasing	Critical Thinking
6			
7			
8			
9			
10			

UNIT THREE

Conquering Niagara Falls

Samuel Dixon walks a tightrope across the Niagrara River in 1890. Dixon was following in the footsteps of the most famous Niagara tightrope walker, Jean Francois Gravelet, known as Blondin. Daredevils have also ridden over the Falls in boats and barrels and jumped from great heights into the swirling waters below.

Most people go to Niagara Falls just to admire the view. They stand on the cliffs and gaze down at the 190-foot waterfalls. They may even shiver when they see the churning whirlpools at the bottom. Most visitors find this experience exciting enough.

2   A few people, however, want more. They want to challenge themselves. And so, over the years, daredevils have tried all kinds of loony stunts at Niagara Falls. They have tried swimming across the Falls. They have tried to steer a boat through the whirlpools. Some have even tumbled over the Falls in a giant rubber ball.

3   The madness began in 1859. An acrobat named Jean François Gravelet came to Niagara Falls. Called Blondin because of his blond hair, he decided he could make some money at the Falls. He arranged to have a cable strung across the river, about 190 feet above the water. On June 30 he prepared to walk from the American side of the Falls to the Canadian side. He would use no safety wire or net. All he wanted was his 38-pound balancing pole, which he would hold in his hands. When people heard of Blondin's plan, they flocked to the water's edge. They paid money to get a seat near the action.

4   As people held their breath, Blondin stepped onto the wire. Slowly he walked farther and farther out over the water. It was 1,200 feet to the other side. For 17½ minutes, Blondin carefully set one foot in front of the other. When he arrived on the far side, people went wild. Blondin became an instant hero.

5   From there, Blondin went on to even greater stunts. One day he pushed a wheelbarrow across the tightrope. On another occasion, he stopped and sipped champagne on the wire. There seemed to be no end to his daring antics. He did a headstand on the wire. He walked across it with baskets on his feet. He even made it across blindfolded.

6   Sometimes, though, things went wrong. One day Blondin carried a chair out over the Falls. He tried to balance the chair on two legs and then sit down on it. The chair wobbled. It fell into the swirling water below. For just a moment, Blondin lost his balance and nearly fell in after the chair.

7   Blondin's craziest stunt came on August 17. He tried to carry his manager across the Falls, piggy-back style. Halfway across, Blondin became tired. Winds kicked up, causing the tightrope to sway. Blondin had trouble moving forward. Sweat broke out on his face. At last, he stopped walking. He set his terrified manager down on the wire next to him. The two men rested for a few minutes. Then Blondin picked the manager up and started moving again. Several times Blondin had to stop and rest. At last he and the manager made it across, but it was a close call.

8   Blondin left Niagara Falls in 1860. But the idea of doing tricks there

lingered on. In 1873 a French man named Ballini jumped 160 feet into the water below the Falls. Amazingly, he survived. In 1886 a Boston policeman named William J. Kendall decided to swim through the whirlpools. He, too, lived to tell about it. Meanwhile, Maria Spelterini followed Blondin's example. She crossed a tightrope over the Falls in 1876.

9 There was still one hurdle to be crossed. No one had ever traveled over the waterfall itself. Or, to be accurate, no one had ever traveled over the waterfall *and lived*. Schoolteacher Anna E. Taylor changed that in 1901. She survived the trip in a barrel. It was not a pleasant experience. By the time she climbed out of the barrel, her head was spinning. She was totally confused. "Did I go over the Falls yet?" she asked.

10 Later, Taylor warned people not to repeat her stunt. "If it was with my dying breath, I would caution anyone against attempting the feat," she said. Then she added, "I will never go over the Falls again. I would sooner walk up to the mouth of a cannon, knowing it was going to blow me to pieces, than make another trip over the Falls."

11 But some people didn't listen to Anna Taylor. They continued to flirt with death at Niagara Falls. Bobby Leach was one of those people. Leach ran a souvenir stand near the Falls. He

bragged to customers about how easy it would be to take a barrel ride over the Falls. People asked him to prove it. And so in 1911, over he went. Leach made it, but he spent six months recuperating from the trip.

12 George Henry Stephen was not so lucky. In 1929 he died trying to go over the Falls. Reports indicated that his oak barrel was "smashed like an egg" by the pounding water. Rescuers saw his tattooed arm floating below the Falls. However, his body was never found.

13 Then there was George Stathakis. This Greek chef went over the Falls in a barrel made of wood and steel. The barrel held together during its plunge, but it became trapped in the whirlpools at the bottom of the Falls. For 22 hours, millions of tons of water crashed down on it. Sometime during those awful hours, Stathakis died.

14 Such deaths haven't stopped the thrill seekers, however. In 1985 John David Munday went over the Falls in a barrel. In 1993 he did it a second time. Munday used a homemade barrel with lots of padding. Even so, his body was cut and bruised during the trip. Rescuers found him passed out inside his barrel. Still, he survived. He became the first person to live through *two* trips over the Falls.

15 Jessie Sharp wanted his name in the record books, too. He hoped to be the

first person to go over the Falls in a canoe. Sharp made his attempt in 1990. He wore no helmet. He used no life jacket or other lifesaving equipment. Explained one friend, "Jessie felt he would stay with the boat. I think he really believed he would make it." Heading over the waterfall, Sharp raised his paddle in the air. Then he disappeared. After 10 minutes, his paddle was seen floating at the bottom of the Falls. An hour later, his battered canoe was found. But Sharp himself was never seen again.

16 What's next? Who knows? But as long as water flows over Niagara Falls, it seems clear that daredevils will always find new ways to challenge themselves there.

If you have been timed while reading this article, enter your reading time below. Then turn to the Words-per-Minute table on page 147 and look up your reading speed (words per minute). Enter your reading speed on the graph on page 148.

Reading Time: Lesson 11

_____ : _____
Minutes   Seconds

A | Finding the Main Idea

One statement below expresses the main idea of the article. One statement is too general, or too broad. The other statement explains only part of the article; it is too narrow. Label the statements using the following key:

M—Main Idea   **B—Too Broad**   **N—Too Narrow**

_____ 1. Niagara Falls is a beautiful and powerful sight as well as a popular tourist attraction.

_____ 2. Niagara Falls has been a magnet for daredevils for more than 100 years.

_____ 3. Acrobat Blondin's first trip across Niagara Falls on a tightrope took 17½ minutes.

_____ Score 15 points for a correct M answer.

_____ Score 5 points for each correct B or N answer.

_____ **Total Score:** Finding the Main Idea

B | Recalling Facts

How well do you remember the facts in the article? Put an X in the box next to the answer that correctly completes each statement about the article.

1. One feat that Blondin did *not* perform on the tightrope over Niagara Falls was
   ☐ a. doing a headstand.
   ☐ b. riding a bicycle.
   ☐ c. carrying another man on his back.

2. When Anna E. Taylor climbed out of the barrel, she
   ☐ a. was dizzy and confused.
   ☐ b. fired a cannon.
   ☐ c. said she wanted to try it again.

3. Before Bobby Leach went over the Falls, he had
   ☐ a. steered a boat through the whirlpools.
   ☐ b. jumped into the water below the Falls.
   ☐ c. run a souvenir stand near the Falls.

4. George Stathakis's trip over the Falls ended when
   ☐ a. the police stopped him from going over.
   ☐ b. his barrel became trapped in whirlpools.
   ☐ c. his barrel was crushed by the pounding water.

5. The only person who twice survived going over the Falls made his trips in a
   ☐ a. padded suit and helmet.
   ☐ b. giant rubber ball.
   ☐ c. padded barrel.

Score 5 points for each correct answer.

_____ **Total Score:** Recalling Facts

C Making Inferences

When you combine your own experience and information from a text to draw a conclusion that is not directly stated in that text, you are making an inference. Below are five statements that may or may not be inferences based on information in the article. Label the statements using the following key:

C—Correct Inference   **F—Faulty Inference**

_____ 1. Some people are willing to put themselves in danger just for excitement.

_____ 2. Before 1901 no one ever thought of trying to go over Niagara Falls.

_____ 3. If someone tried to walk a tightrope over Niagara Falls today, probably no one would bother to watch.

_____ 4. In the last 20 years, it has become easier and less risky to travel over Niagara Falls.

_____ 5. Whether you live or die, going over Niagara Falls is pretty much a matter of luck.

Score 5 points for each correct answer.

_____ **Total Score:** Making Inferences

D Using Words Precisely

Each numbered sentence below contains an underlined word or phrase from the article. Following the sentence are three definitions. One definition is closest to the meaning of the underlined word. One definition is opposite or nearly opposite. Label those two definitions using the following key; do not label the remaining definition.

C—Closest   **O—Opposite or Nearly Opposite**

1. They may even shiver when they see the <u>churning</u> whirlpools at the bottom.

_____ a. swirling

_____ b. magical

_____ c. calm

2. And so, over the years, daredevils have tried all kinds of <u>loony</u> stunts at Niagara Falls.

_____ a. sensible

_____ b. foolish

_____ c. expensive

3. Or, to be <u>accurate</u>, no one had ever traveled over the waterfall and lived.

_____ a. wrong

_____ b. kind

_____ c. exactly correct

4. Leach made it, but he spent six months <u>recuperating</u> from the trip.

_____ a. writing about experiences

_____ b. returning to health

_____ c. becoming worse

5. The barrel held together during its <u>plunge</u>, but it became trapped in the whirlpools at the bottom of the Falls.

_____ a. sudden drop

_____ b. rise

_____ c. trick

_____ Score 3 points for each correct C answer.

_____ Score 2 points for each correct O answer.

_____ **Total Score:** Using Words Precisely

Enter the four total scores in the spaces below, and add them together to find your Reading Comprehension Score. Then record your score on the graph on page 149.

Score	Question Type	Lesson 11
_____	Finding the Main Idea	
_____	Recalling Facts	
_____	Making Inferences	
_____	Using Words Precisely	
_____	**Reading Comprehension Score**	

Author's Approach

Put an X in the box next to the correct answer.

1. The main purpose of the first paragraph is to

☐ a. explain why most people are afraid of Niagara Falls.

☐ b. describe Niagara Falls.

☐ c. persuade readers to go to Niagara Falls.

2. In this article, "As people held their breath, Blondin stepped onto the wire" means

☐ a. nervous spectators paid close attention when Blondin began his tightrope act.

☐ b. spectators were asked to be quiet when Blondin stepped onto the wire.

☐ c. spectators were not too interested in Blondin's act.

3. The authors probably wrote this article to

☐ a. introduce the reader to Blondin.

☐ b. persuade tourists to visit Niagara Falls.

☐ c. inform the reader about daredevils' attempts to conquer Niagara Falls.

4. The authors tell this story mainly by

☐ a. describing events in the order they happened.

☐ b. comparing different topics.

☐ c. using their imagination and creativity.

_____ Number of correct answers

Record your personal assessment of your work on the Critical Thinking Chart on page 150.

Summarizing and Paraphrasing

Put an X in the box next to the correct answer for questions
1 and 3. Follow the directions provided for question 2.

1. Below are summaries of the article. Choose the summary that
   says all the most important things about the article but in the
   fewest words.

   ☐ a. Niagara Falls is one of the most unusual sights on the
          North American continent. Waters from the Niagara River
          fall 190 feet to the bottom of the Falls, where they churn
          around in dangerous whirlpools. Most people are amazed
          at the awesome power of Niagara Falls.

   ☐ b. Blondin was the first famous acrobat to tightrope walk over
          Niagara Falls. At various times, his act included pushing a
          wheelbarrow across the wire, doing a headstand on the
          wire, and carrying another person high above the Falls.

   ☐ c. Daredevils have been pitting their courage against the
          power of Niagara Falls for years. Some have walked the
          high wire above the Falls, and others have gone over the
          Falls in barrels. Niagara Falls will continue to fascinate thrill
          seekers for years to come.

2. Reread paragraph 10 in the article. Below, write a summary of
   the paragraph in no more than 25 words.

   _____

   _____

   _____

Reread your summary and decide whether it covers the
important ideas in the paragraph. Next, decide how to shorten
the summary to 15 words or less without leaving out any
essential information. Write this summary below.

_____

_____

_____

3. Choose the sentence that correctly restates the following
   sentence from the article: "In 1873 a French man named
   Ballini jumped 160 feet into the water below the Falls."

   ☐ a. In 1873 a French man jumped into the river water swirling
          below the Falls.

   ☐ b. Ballini, a French man, leaped from the top of the Falls into
          the water below—a jump of 160 feet—in 1873.

   ☐ c. A French man who was below the Falls jumped into the
          water in 1873 and swam 160 feet.

   +--+
   | |
   | _____ Number of correct answers |
   | |
   | Record your personal assessment of your work on the |
   | Critical Thinking Chart on page 150. |
   | |
   +--+

Critical Thinking

Follow the directions provided for questions 1, 3, and 5. Put an X in the box next to the correct answer for the other questions.

1. For each statement below, write *O* if it expresses an opinion or write *F* if it expresses a fact.

   _____ a. Both Blondin and Maria Spelterini crossed above Niagara Falls on a tightrope.

   _____ b. Blondin was the greatest of the daredevils who challenged the power of Niagara Falls.

   _____ c. The most ridiculous way to go over the Falls was in a canoe.

2. Judging by the events in the article, you can predict that the following will happen next:

   ☐ a. Someone will think of a new way of traveling over the Falls and will try it.

   ☐ b. No one else will ever try to go over the Falls.

   ☐ c. The next person to ride a canoe over the Falls, without wearing a helmet or a life jacket, will make the trip safely and easily.

3. Choose from the letters below to correctly complete the following statement. Write the letters on the lines.

   In the article, _____ and _____ are different.

   a. the outcome of daredevil Anna Taylor's trip over the Falls

   b. the outcome of daredevil George Henry Stephen's trip over the Falls

   c. the outcome of daredevil George Stathakis's trip over the Falls

4. What was the cause of George Stathakis's death?

   ☐ a. His barrel fell apart during the trip over the Falls.

   ☐ b. His barrel became trapped in the whirlpools at the bottom of the Falls.

   ☐ c. His barrel was lost in the Niagara River.

5. In which paragraph did you find your information or details to answer question 4? _____

_____ Number of correct answers

Record your personal assessment of your work on the Critical Thinking Chart on page 150.

Personal Response

I wonder why _____

_____

_____

_____

Self-Assessment

While reading the article, I found it easiest to _____

_____

_____

_____

Extreme Biking

They look like aliens from a Star Wars movie. They wear body armor from their shoulders down to their shins. Thick pads shield their chests, hips, arms, and legs. The special gloves they wear have padding on each finger. On their heads, they display space-age helmets designed to protect the face as well as the head. Meet the daredevils known as downhill mountain bike racers.

Racing down mountains at speeds of up to 60 miles per hour provides enough danger to keep even these downhill mountain bikers happy. Extreme bikers are used to falling and breaking a few bones. When their bodies heal, extreme bikers climb right back on their bikes.

2   Only the most gutsy athletes even dream of racing downhill on a bike at speeds approaching 60 miles per hour. Biking that fast down a nice paved road would be scary enough. But imagine hopping over ruts, rocks, and tree stumps. Just think about getting a flat tire or a derailed chain along the way. Or picture yourself sliding on some wet grass or mud, missing a turn, and smashing into a tree. The dangers of this sport make most people wonder why riders don't wear even more padding.

3   The sport of downhill biking is filled with offbeat characters. There seems to be something about this activity that attracts them. They are not like professional athletes in most other sports. They don't talk the same, and they don't dress the same. You won't find their pictures on cereal boxes either.

4   These athletes live on the edge. They thrive on danger. They know they are just a wrong turn or an unseen bump away from the next bad fall. That risk, of course, is what mountain bike riders love about the sport.

5   Missy "The Missile" Giove is a case in point. Giove has always been a thrill-seeker. Growing up in New York City, she got a job delivering Chinese food at the age of 14. She did it on her bike. Biking on busy streets in the city is always risky. Luckily, Giove rode a heavy bike, because she "got hit by a lot of taxis."

6   When it came to sports, Giove would try anything if there was danger involved. For a while she trained to be a ski racer. She also tried rock climbing, snowboarding, wrestling, and roller hockey. She didn't discover mountain racing until 1990. A friend dared her to enter a race at Mount Snow in Vermont. Giove took the challenge. After that one race she fell in love with downhill racing. A few months later she was riding against the best women in the world.

7   As a downhill biker, Giove sports a unique look. Let's begin with the hair. She wears a buzzcut on the top of her head. Along each side, she has dreadlocks dangling down. As an added touch, she has dyed sections of her hair different colors. Giove wears a gold nose ring and a half dozen earrings. In addition, she has a tattoo of the Road Runner on her ankle. "He's kind of like a symbol for me," she once explained. "He's fast."

8   But Giove is best known for her weird necklace. For years she has worn a dried piranha on a rope. (A piranha is a small fish best known for its razor-sharp teeth and huge appetite.) Giove says the necklace reminds her "to be aggressive, to just act on instinct."

9   Missy Giove's aggressiveness has led to an all-or-nothing racing style. She usually wins her races—if she doesn't hit a tree. Even when she crashes, she often crawls back to her bike just to finish the race. It is because she rides so fast that Giove has been given the nickname "The Missile." During the 1990s, she was the top female rider in the world.

10 Giove is also one of the most frequently injured riders. "I broke my left wrist three times and my right wrist twice," she said. She has suffered more cracked ribs than she can count. She ripped the muscles in her shoulder. She also shattered a foot,

a kneecap, several teeth, and a collarbone. A broken pelvic bone put her in a wheelchair for three months.

11   Still, she kept coming back for more. In 1996, after the broken pelvic bone, she won the World Cup biking title for the second time. As her father and manager said, "The body mends. She wasn't raised a sissy."

12   As bikers like Giove know, downhill racing isn't just dangerous—it's grueling. It takes raw strength to control a bike at such high speeds. And that control has to be held all the way down a three- or four-mile course. "To do this and be able to hang on and not fall off and not get fatigued," Missy Giove says, "makes it one of the most physically demanding sports."

13   A rider also needs to be mentally tough. Clearly, this is not a sport for people who need time to make up their minds. Boulders, tree roots, and other hazards appear with only split-second warning. There really isn't any time to think at all. Decisions are based on guts and instinct. A rider just sees and reacts.

14   "When I have a good race," Giove once declared, "I don't remember what went on."

15   That doesn't mean riders don't get scared. Giove has acknowledged that she feels fear. People may think she is crazy, but she isn't *that* crazy. "You never conquer your fear," she says. "You have to work with it, because it's always going to be there. If you weren't afraid, then it wouldn't be fun."

16   As if downhill mountain biking wasn't hard enough, someone came up with the idea of adding snow. The resulting sport is called Biker X. It was added to the 1999 Winter X Games. (The X stands for "extreme.") Six riders race each other down a snow-covered mountain. The course is laced with jumps and steep, banked turns. Each rider fights to get the best line down. "The first time I went down, it was really scary," said one woman rider.

17   Even Missy Giove was a bit shaken by the wild Biker X competition. "It was full-on carnage out there. I got [hit] in the air and crashed."

18   Even without the snow, downhill biking is a really loony sport. That's why it's so popular among TV spectators. "Downhill racing is the future of the sport," says Giove. Other forms of bike racing are too tame for TV. As Giove says, "America likes to see people crash."

If you have been timed while reading this article, enter your reading time below. Then turn to the Words-per-Minute table on page 147 and look up your reading speed (words per minute). Enter your reading speed on the graph on page 148.

Reading Time: Lesson 12

_____ : _____
Minutes   Seconds

A Finding the Main Idea

One statement below expresses the main idea of the article. One statement is too general, or too broad. The other statement explains only part of the article; it is too narrow. Label the statements using the following key:

M—Main Idea   **B—Too Broad**   **N—Too Narrow**

_____ 1. Downhill biker Missy Giove has been injured many times; she has suffered broken wrists, kneecaps, teeth, collarbone, and pelvic bone.

_____ 2. Fans of downhill biking are attracted by the danger of the sport.

_____ 3. Downhill biking, in which bikers race downhill at speeds of about 60 miles per hour, attracts freethinking daredevils.

_____ Score 15 points for a correct M answer.

_____ Score 5 points for each correct B or N answer.

_____ **Total Score:** Finding the Main Idea

B Recalling Facts

How well do you remember the facts in the article? Put an X in the box next to the answer that correctly completes each statement about the article.

1. Missy Giove's first job was
   ☐ a. selling newspapers in New York City.
   ☐ b. selling bicycles in New York City.
   ☐ c. delivering Chinese food in New York City.

2. Missy Giove's nickname is
   ☐ a. "The Madwoman."
   ☐ b. "The Missile."
   ☐ c. "Mighty."

3. Giove's necklace is a
   ☐ a. piranha on a rope.
   ☐ b. bottlecap on a fishline.
   ☐ c. bike chain.

4. The X in Biker X games stands for
   ☐ a. "extreme."
   ☐ b. "exciting."
   ☐ c. "exhausting."

5. Biker X is a form of downhill biking done in
   ☐ a. mud.
   ☐ b. sand.
   ☐ c. snow.

Score 5 points for each correct answer.

_____ **Total Score:** Recalling Facts

C | Making Inferences

When you combine your own experience with information from a text to draw a conclusion that is not directly stated in that text, you are making an inference. Below are five statements that may or may not be inferences based on information in the article. Label the statements using the following key:

C—Correct Inference   **F—Faulty Inference**

_____ 1. In order to be successful at downhill biking, you must be an offbeat dresser and thinker.

_____ 2. Downhill bikers probably spend a lot of time in hospital emergency rooms.

_____ 3. Downhill biking requires both upper-body and lower-body strength.

_____ 4. Before the race downhill bikers carefully plan their paths down a course.

_____ 5. Most TV viewers don't like to see athletes hurt in any competition.

Score 5 points for each correct answer.

_____ **Total Score:** Making Inferences

D | Using Words Precisely

Each numbered sentence below contains an underlined word or phrase from the article. Following the sentence are three definitions. One definition is closest to the meaning of the underlined word. One definition is opposite or nearly opposite. Label those two definitions using the following key; do not label the remaining definition.

C—Closest   **O—Opposite or Nearly Opposite**

1. Only the most <u>gutsy</u> athletes even dream of racing downhill on a bike at speeds approaching 60 miles per hour.

_____ a. experienced

_____ b. cowardly

_____ c. courageous

2. The sport of downhill biking is filled with <u>offbeat</u> characters.

_____ a. weird

_____ b. friendly

_____ c. normal

3. They <u>thrive on</u> danger.

_____ a. are ruined by

_____ b. do well in

_____ c. seek

4. As a downhill biker, Giove sports a <u>unique</u> look.

_____ a. one-of-a-kind

_____ b. comical

_____ c. common

5. Giove has <u>acknowledged</u> that she feels fear.

_____ a. proven

_____ b. admitted

_____ c. denied

_____ Score 3 points for each correct C answer.

_____ Score 2 points for each correct O answer.

_____ **Total Score:** Using Words Precisely

Enter the four total scores in the spaces below, and add them together to find your Reading Comprehension Score. Then record your score on the graph on page 149.

Score	Question Type	Lesson 12
_____	Finding the Main Idea	
_____	Recalling Facts	
_____	Making Inferences	
_____	Using Words Precisely	
_____	**Reading Comprehension Score**	

Author's Approach

Put an X in the box next to the correct answer.

1. The main purpose of the first paragraph is to

☐ a. describe the appearance of downhill bikers.

☐ b. make fun of downhill bikers.

☐ c. create a silly mood.

2. From the statements below, choose those that you believe the authors would agree with.

☐ a. Downhill bikers never feel fear before they begin a race.

☐ b. Downhill bikers must be very strong.

☐ c. Downhill mountain bike racers look different from most other athletes.

3. Judging by statements from the article "Extreme Biking," you can conclude that the author wants the reader to think that

☐ a. Missy Giove's father is proud of her.

☐ b. Missy Giove's father can't understand why his daughter risks her safety with downhill biking.

☐ c. Missy Giove's father wants her to stop downhill biking as soon as possible.

4. Choose the statement below that best describes the authors' position in paragraph 16.

☐ a. It is ridiculous to race downhill in the snow.

☐ b. Biker X is unnecessarily dangerous and should be stopped.

☐ c. Biker X is even harder than downhill mountain bike racing.

_____ Number of correct answers

Record your personal assessment of your work on the Critical Thinking Chart on page 150.

Summarizing and Paraphrasing

Follow the directions provided for question 1. Put an X in the box next to the correct answer for the other questions.

1. Reread paragraph 13 in the article. Below, write a summary of the paragraph in no more than 25 words.

_____

_____

_____

Reread your summary and decide whether it covers the important ideas in the paragraph. Next, decide how to shorten the summary to 15 words or less without leaving out any essential information. Write this summary below.

_____

_____

_____

2. Read the statement from the article below. Then read the paraphrase of that statement. Choose the reason that best tells why the paraphrase does not say the same thing as the statement.

   Statement: Biker X, a form of downhill mountain biking done in the snow, was added to the 1999 Winter X Games.

   Paraphrase: The 1999 Winter Games added the version of downhill mountain biking that is done in the snow to its scheduled competitions.

☐ a. Paraphrase says too much.

☐ b. Paraphrase doesn't say enough.

☐ c. Paraphrase doesn't agree with the statement.

3. Choose the sentence that correctly restates the following sentence from the article: "As bikers like Giove know, downhill racing isn't just dangerous—it's grueling."

☐ a. Bikers know that in addition to being dangerous, downhill biking is also exhausting.

☐ b. Most bikers hate downhill racing because it is so dangerous and grueling.

☐ c. Most bikers admit that being grueling is even worse than being dangerous.

_____ Number of correct answers

Record your personal assessment of your work on the Critical Thinking Chart on page 150.

CRITICAL THINKING

Critical Thinking

Put an X in the box next to the correct answer for questions 1 and 4. Follow the directions provided for the other questions.

1. Which of the following statements from the article is an opinion rather than a fact?

☐ a. A friend dared her to enter a race at Mount Snow in Vermont.

☐ b. Only the most gutsy athletes even dream of racing downhill on a bike at speeds approaching 60 miles per hour.

☐ c. A broken pelvic bone put her in a wheelchair for three months.

2. Choose from the letters below to correctly complete the following statement. Write the letters on the lines.

   In the article, _____ and _____ are alike.

   a. Missy Giove's appearance

   b. most professional athletes' appearance

   c. many downhill mountain bikers' appearance

3. Read paragraph 8. Then choose from the letters below to correctly complete the following statement. Write the letters on the lines.

   According to paragraph 8, _____ because _____.

   a. the piranha is a fish

   b. Missy Giove wears a piranha on a rope around her neck

   c. the piranha reminds her to be aggressive

4. What did you have to do to answer question 1?

☐ a. find an opinion (what someone thinks about something)

☐ b. find a description (how something looks)

☐ c. find a contrast (how things are different)

_____ Number of correct answers

Record your personal assessment of your work on the Critical Thinking Chart on page 150.

Personal Response

Why do you think Missy Giove went back to downhill mountain biking so quickly after recovering from a serious accident?

_____

_____

_____

Self-Assessment

From reading this article, I have learned _____

_____

_____

_____

Buzkashi: War on Horseback

What is Afghanistan's national sport? If you guessed soccer, wrestling, or any other common activity, you're wrong. In Afghanistan the national sport is no ordinary game. The name itself should give you a clue. It is *buzkashi*, which means "goat grabbing."

2   Buzkashi has a long history. It began nearly 800 years ago. That was when a famous Afghan leader named Genghis Khan led an army of soldiers on horseback. Khan and his men conquered lands from China to Europe. Khan's soldiers were the finest horsemen in the world. They could mount at a moment's notice. They could ride all day. These brutal warriors could attack and fight without ever getting off their horses.

3   To keep their riding skills sharp, the horsemen played a special game. They tried to scoop up an object while riding a horse at high speeds. In those days, the object they grabbed was the body of a dead enemy. Today, a human corpse is no longer used. But the game lives on. The only difference is that now buzkashi players use the headless body of a goat.

4   Before the game begins, the players mount their horses. There are usually two or three teams made up of several horsemen each. The total number of players can range from about 10 to 100. The object of the game is pretty simple. The goat, called the *buz,* is put into a ditch. On a given signal—often a rifle shot or a whistle—all the horsemen rush to the ditch. Each one tries to grab the goat and lift it onto his saddle.

5   The one who gets the goat races off. With one hand grasping the goat and the other handling the reins, this horseman may end up holding his whip between his teeth. He tries to gallop down the field, around a pole, and back to the ditch, where he then drops the goat. If he manages to do all this, his team scores a point.

6   Right from the beginning, the riders on the other teams try to wrestle the buz away from him. They'll do whatever it takes to get that goat. The results are often violent. Riders and horses get knocked all over the place. Even the horses kick and bite each other. The fighting for the buz is so fierce that the body of the goat may get torn to pieces. If that happens, another one is brought out to replace it.

7   In his book *The Horsemen,* Joseph Kessel describes the start of one game. "Silently, step by step, the sixty horsemen [surround] the hole that [holds] the slaughtered beast." The players, wearing team colors, form a circle. Then the horses explode toward each other. Kessel writes that the field turns into "an enormous whirlwind." The air is filled with "whoops, oaths, wordless threats, . . . lashing whips ripping into muzzles and faces." The riders fight as if their lives depend on it.

Lucky and skillful players among the hundreds on the buzkashi field close in on the spot where the buz—*the body of a goat—lies. Whoever gets close enough will reach down, grab the heavy body, and try to carry it across the field at a gallop.*

They struggle with "their faces in the dust, their nails clawing . . . to find the headless goat, grasp it, and snatch it up."

8   At times there is nothing to see but a huge cloud of dust. Then, suddenly, one rider emerges with the buz. A second later, the others are charging after him. If they catch him, the battle for the goat begins anew.

9   When a point is finally scored, there is a break in the game. Money or gifts are awarded to the winning rider. The contest usually doesn't end until all the prize money and gifts have been given out. So some games last all day.

10   To be successful, players need good horses. Horses are bred especially to play buzkashi, and good ones cost a lot of money. When a buzkashi colt is born, its feet are not allowed to touch the ground. According to an Afghan tradition, touching the earth too soon would cause the colt to lose its "wings." Later, the young colts are trained to dodge and attack at the rider's command. They are also trained not to step on a fallen rider. That explains how such a rough sport can have so few serious injuries.

11   The Afghans love their buzkashi horses. They will spend years training them. The best ones last up to 20 years as buzkashi mounts. In fact, many people in Afghanistan regard the horses more highly than the riders. They often say, "Better to have a poor rider on a good horse than a good rider on a poor horse."

12   Best of all, of course, is to have both a good horse *and* a good rider. It takes a long, long time to become a top rider. Young boys spend years training in their villages. They must develop incredible balance and a keen sense of timing. In addition, they must be very strong, since the buz alone often weighs close to a 100 pounds. Most riders don't reach the top of their game until they are in their late 30s or early 40s.

13   Buzkashi is a serious sport. It isn't the kind of contest where you shake hands at the end. There is too much pride involved. And if winning brings pride, losing brings shame. One Afghan said, "It is better to shoot a [man] with a gun straight in the face than to tell him loudly on the buzkashi field that his horse is weak and not fast enough."

14   In 1955 Afghanistan made buzkashi an official sport. That meant setting some clear-cut rules. These rules cover such things as the shape of the field, scoring, and the size of the teams. The rules provide for a regular season with playoffs and a championship. The rules also try to tone down the violence. Mounted referees can call two kinds of fouls. One is for whipping a player on purpose. The other is for pulling a rider off his horse.

15   Buzkashi, however, is too important to be played only by the best players. Anyone can set up a match. All you need is someone who can offer money or prizes. So unofficial games are still played all the time. And they are played the old-fashioned way—war on horseback with no rules.

If you have been timed while reading this article, enter your reading time below. Then turn to the Words-per-Minute table on page 147 and look up your reading speed (words per minute). Enter your reading speed on the graph on page 148.

Reading Time: Lesson 13

—————— : ——————
Minutes   *Seconds*

A | Finding the Main Idea

One statement below expresses the main idea of the article. One statement is too general, or too broad. The other statement explains only part of the article; it is too narrow. Label the statements using the following key:

M—Main Idea   **B—Too Broad**   **N—Too Narrow**

_____ 1. In the warlike game of buzkashi, teams of men on horseback struggle with each other to pick up the body of a goat and carry it across a field.

_____ 2. Afghanistan's national sport, buzkashi, or "goat grabbing," is no ordinary game.

_____ 3. The goat's body used in Afghanistan's buzkashi game replaces the human body used by Genghis Khan's warriors.

_____ Score 15 points for a correct M answer.

_____ Score 5 points for each correct B or N answer.

_____ **Total Score:** Finding the Main Idea

B | Recalling Facts

How well do you remember the facts in the article? Put an X in the box next to the answer that correctly completes each statement about the article.

1. Buzkashi began nearly 800 years ago when
   - ☐ a. the game became Afghanistan's national sport.
   - ☐ b. Genghis Khan's warriors were conquering lands from China to Europe.
   - ☐ c. Afghanistan took on its modern borders.

2. Centuries ago, warriors played buzkashi to
   - ☐ a. relax after a hard day of fighting.
   - ☐ b. win money in professional competitions.
   - ☐ c. keep their fighting and riding skills sharp.

3. The number of players on the field at once
   - ☐ a. is limited to 10.
   - ☐ b. is never more than 50.
   - ☐ c. may range up to 100 or so.

4. As play begins, every horseman tries to
   - ☐ a. pick up the headless body of a goat.
   - ☐ b. show how fast he can ride straight ahead.
   - ☐ c. get the attention of the spectators.

5. The horses ridden in a buzkashi game are
   - ☐ a. assigned to riders by a lottery.
   - ☐ b. well trained and quick to react.
   - ☐ c. usually worn out after two years or so.

Score 5 points for each correct answer.

_____ **Total Score:** Recalling Facts

C | Making Inferences

When you combine your own experience and information from a text to draw a conclusion that is not directly stated in that text, you are making an inference. Below are five statements that may or may not be inferences based on information in the article. Label the statements using the following key:

C—Correct Inference　　　　**F—Faulty Inference**

_____ 1. Many people in Afghanistan live in the country or in villages where they can own horses.

_____ 2. Buzkashi did not have clear-cut, official rules before 1955.

_____ 3. The man who first picks up the goat's body is usually the one who scores a point.

_____ 4. A buzkashi rider must pay a great deal for a horse that is good in buzkashi.

_____ 5. A buzkashi player would consider the American game of professional football as overly rough.

Score 5 points for each correct answer.

_____ **Total Score:** Making Inferences

D | Using Words Precisely

Each numbered sentence below contains an underlined word or phrase from the article. Following the sentence are three definitions. One definition is closest to the meaning of the underlined word. One definition is opposite or nearly opposite. Label those two definitions using the following key; do not label the remaining definition.

C—Closest　　　　**O—Opposite or Nearly Opposite**

1. Khan and his men <u>conquered</u> lands from China to Europe.

_____ a. visited

_____ b. took by force

_____ c. gave up

2. They tried to <u>scoop up</u> an object while riding a horse at high speeds.

_____ a. drop

_____ b. identify

_____ c. pick up

3. Silently, step by step, the 60 horsemen [surround] the hole that [holds] the <u>slaughtered</u> beast.

_____ a. killed

_____ b. hidden

_____ c. revived; restored

4. At times there is nothing to see but a huge cloud of dust. Then, suddenly, one rider <u>emerges</u> with the buz.

_____ a. stands

_____ b. comes out

_____ c. goes in

5. Young boys spend years training in their villages. They must develop <u>incredible</u> balance and a keen sense of timing.

_____ a. extraordinary

_____ b. barely adequate

_____ c. changeable

_____ Score 3 points for each correct C answer.

_____ Score 2 points for each correct O answer.

_____ **Total Score:** Using Words Precisely

Enter the four total scores in the spaces below, and add them together to find your Reading Comprehension Score. Then record your score on the graph on page 149.

Score	Question Type	Lesson 13
_____	Finding the Main Idea	
_____	Recalling Facts	
_____	Making Inferences	
_____	Using Words Precisely	
_____	**Reading Comprehension Score**	

Author's Approach

Put an X in the box next to the correct answer.

1. What is the authors' purpose in writing "Buzkashi: War on Horseback"?

☐ a. to encourage the reader to travel to Afghanistan

☐ b. to inform the reader about a unique, exciting game

☐ d. to emphasize the similarities between buzkashi and polo

2. From the statements below, choose those that you believe the authors would agree with.

☐ a. Buzkashi is an ancient game with a proud tradition.

☐ b. Buzkashi would be a popular sport in the United States.

☐ c. Buzkashi is a violent game.

3. Judging by statements from the article, you can conclude that the authors want the reader to think that

☐ a. most people in Afghanistan believe that buzkashi is too violent and they want it stopped.

☐ b. many buzkashi players feel that the best way to play the game is with no rules.

☐ c. only young people enjoy buzkashi.

4. What do the authors imply by saying "In fact, many people in Afghanistan regard the horses more highly than the riders"?

☐ a. People in Afghanistan realize that a good horse is essential for winning at buzkashi.

☐ b. People in Afghanistan have no respect for buzkashi players.

☐ c. People in Afghanistan love all animals, but especially horses.

_____ Number of correct answers

Record your personal assessment of your work on the Critical Thinking Chart on page 150.

Summarizing and Paraphrasing

Put an X in the box next to the correct answer for the following questions.

1. Below are summaries of the article. Choose the summary that says all the most important things about the article but in the fewest words.

   ☐ a. Horses that are used in buzkashi are valued even more than the players themselves. They are treated specially from birth and are trained carefully. Buzkashi horses are worth a great deal of money in Afghanistan.

   ☐ b. Buzkashi began almost 800 years ago when horsemen in Genghis Khan's army were looking for a way to sharpen their riding skills. It is still popular in Afghanistan today.

   ☐ c. Buzkashi, the national sport of Afghanistan, is a violent game in which players riding fast horses try to scoop up and carry the body of a goat to score points. There are no set rules for the game.

2. Read the statement from the article below. Then read the paraphrase of that statement. Choose the reason that best tells why the paraphrase does not say the same thing as the statement.

   Statement: Buzkashi players are often most effective during their 40s or 50s—at a time when most other athletes have retired from their games.

   Paraphrase: Most buzkashi players retire from the game in their 40s or 50s, just like athletes in other games.

   ☐ a. Paraphrase says too much.

   ☐ b. Paraphrase doesn't say enough.

   ☐ c. Paraphrase doesn't agree with the statement.

3. Choose the sentence that correctly restates the following sentence from the article: "Later, the young colts are trained to dodge and attack at the rider's command."

   ☐ a. Colts are trained to dodge and attack the rider on command.

   ☐ b. Later, trainers teach the colts to obey the rider's commands to dodge and attack.

   ☐ c. The rider trains his colts to decide when to dodge or attack.

_____ Number of correct answers

Record your personal assessment of your work on the Critical Thinking Chart on page 150.

Critical Thinking

Put an X in the box next to the correct answer for questions 1 and 2. Follow the directions provided for the other questions.

1. Which of the following statements from the article is an opinion rather than a fact?

   ☐ a. In 1955 Afghanistan made buzkashi an official sport.

   ☐ b. There are usually two or three teams made up of several horsemen each.

   ☐ c. Buzkashi, however, is too important to be played only by the best players.

2. From what the article told about the importance that Afghans place on buzkashi, you can predict that

☐ a. Afghans will continue to play buzkashi for a long time to come.

☐ b. modern team sports such as soccer and basketball will soon become more popular than buzkashi.

☐ c. buzkashi will be declared illegal in Afghanistan.

3. Read paragraphs 2 and 3. Then choose from the letters below to correctly complete the following statement. Write the letters on the lines.

According to paragraphs 2 and 3, _____ because _____.

a. Genghis Khan's horsemen wanted to keep their riding skills sharp

b. Genghis Khan's horsemen played buzkashi

c. Genghis Khan's horsemen could ride all day

4. Which paragraphs from the article provide evidence that supports your answer to question 3? _____

_____ Number of correct answers

Record your personal assessment of your work on the Critical Thinking Chart on page 150.

Personal Response

If you could ask the author of the article one question, what would it be?

_____

_____

_____

Self-Assessment

When reading the article, I was having trouble with _____

_____

_____

_____

BASE Jumping

You're watching a crime in progress. Jumping off **B**uildings, **A**ntennae, bridge **S**pans, and **E**arthbound objects—also known as BASE jumping—is illegal throughout the United States. These BASE jumpers are leaping off buildings in downtown Los Angeles. Once they land, they could be arrested.

On October 18, 1990, a young man walked into St. Paul's Cathedral in London, England. He began to climb the stairs to the Whispering Gallery that stands 102 feet above the cathedral floor. No one paid any attention to this man or to the friend who was with him. No one noticed the parachute the man wore on his back.

2   Soon the young man reached the gallery. He climbed over the safety railing. Then, to the astonishment of

everyone in the church, he jumped. The friend who was with him stayed in the gallery and pulled the rip cord on the parachute. (The jumper wouldn't have had time to open it himself.) As the man floated to the floor, he almost hit a woman. He landed, then scrambled out of his parachute and ran away before police could arrest him.

3   The unknown man was a BASE jumper. That's someone who parachutes from a low level. The term *BASE* refers to the objects such a person jumps from: *B*uildings, *A*ntennae, bridge *S*pans, and other *E*arthbound objects. More and more people are taking up this sport. They are parachuting off cliffs, towers, bridges—and just about anything else that juts up into the air.

4   BASE jumping is far more risky than normal parachuting. First, there is the danger of smacking into the side of the object from which you have jumped. Second, when you jump from a plane there is lots of time to open your parachute. But when you jump from a building or cliff, you have just a few seconds.

5   Finally, when you jump from a plane you have *two* parachutes. If the first one doesn't open, you still have another one to try. In BASE jumping you don't have enough time to open a second chute. So there's no point in wearing one. If the one chute you have doesn't work, that's all there is to it. On the plus side, at least you don't have long to worry about what's ahead!

6   For most people, regular parachuting is an extreme sport. So, too, is mountain biking and high-speed in-line skating. But these sports don't cut it any more with BASE jumpers. In their opinion, the risk of a bloody nose or a scraped knee isn't enough to make a sport "extreme." For BASE jumpers, there has to be a real chance that you'll die. As BASE jumper Mike Steele said, "We have redefined what makes for a daring and dangerous adventure. Now it takes more effort to be extreme."

7   So BASE jumpers look for wild places from which to leap. One popular spot is Angel Falls in Venezuela. At 3,212 feet, it is the highest waterfall in the world. Jan Davis, a grandmother, once jumped there. The fact that she could have been mangled or killed didn't seem to bother her. "I have nothing to prove to anyone," she said. "I do it because I enjoy it."

8   More than 30 BASE jumpers have died since the sport began. In fact, the sport is so dangerous it is banned throughout the United States. Exceptions are granted only for a few special occasions. Still, people break the law and keep BASE jumping anyway. "It's definitely an underground thing," said one BASE jumper. "You get in so much trouble for even thinking about doing it."

9   The Royal Gorge Bridge in Colorado is 1,053 feet high. It is the highest suspension bridge in the world. That makes it an attraction for BASE jumpers. A Colorado state law prohibits people from jumping off the bridge. But every year, two or three people try it. "We catch some; some get away," said police lieutenant Steve McLaury.

10   Donald Samson knew it was illegal. Still, in 1994 he decided to jump off the Royal Gorge Bridge. Something went terribly wrong with Samson's leap. He died from severe head injuries. The police don't know for sure what went wrong. Lieutenant McLaury

suggested that Samson might have been caught in a wind shift. That could have caused him to slam into the rocks on the way down. Maybe he didn't open his chute fast enough. Or perhaps the chute itself didn't work properly. In any case, at the age of 26, Donald Samson joined the ranks of dead BASE jumpers.

11 Alf Humphries was 49 when he made his last jump. Humphries had plenty of experience. He had skydived more than 2,800 times. He had BASE jumped 130 times, including a leap off the Royal Gorge Bridge. Humphries had even plunged off the roofs of office buildings in Los Angeles and Denver.

12 In 1993 Humphries tried an "easy" jump off a 950-foot tower in Colorado. But nothing about BASE jumping is easy. Humphries understood that. Some of his friends had been badly injured BASE jumping. Humphries himself had broken his knees, legs, ankles, and feet. But this time it was much worse. His parachute didn't open all the way. It slowed him down enough so that he wasn't killed. But Humphries hit the ground so hard he broke his spine. As a result, he will spend the rest of his life in a wheelchair.

13 Humphries now wishes he hadn't taken up BASE jumping. He advises others not to do it. As Humphries said, "Life is not as much fun as it was." But others continue to jump, regardless of the risks. As Scott Chew, a friend of Humphries, said, "[BASE jumping] is just like any other sport. People don't stop riding bicycles just because they read about other people falling off bicycles." On the other hand, when someone falls off a bicycle, people don't talk about outlawing the sport. And they usually don't need to bury the biker.

If you have been timed while reading this article, enter your reading time below. Then turn to the Words-per-Minute table on page 147 and look up your reading speed (words per minute). Enter your reading speed on the graph on page 148.

Reading Time: Lesson 14

_____ : _____
Minutes   *Seconds*

A | Finding the Main Idea

One statement below expresses the main idea of the article. One statement is too general, or too broad. The other statement explains only part of the article; it is too narrow. Label the statements using the following key:

M—Main Idea   B—Too Broad   N—Too Narrow

_____ 1. A BASE jumper uses only one parachute, since there isn't enough time to try a second one.

_____ 2. BASE jumping is a dangerous way to get a thrill, as proved by the number of people who have been injured or even killed while attempting it.

_____ 3. BASE jumping is a popular extreme sport in many parts of the world.

_____ Score 15 points for a correct M answer.

_____ Score 5 points for each correct B or N answer.

_____ **Total Score:** Finding the Main Idea

B | Recalling Facts

How well do you remember the facts in the article? Put an X in the box next to the answer that correctly completes each statement about the article.

1. The BASE jumper at St. Paul's Cathedral
   ☐ a. was immediately arrested.
   ☐ b. was taken to the nearest hospital.
   ☐ c. ran away before the police arrived.

2. Every BASE jumper needs
   ☐ a. a parachute.
   ☐ b. a life jacket.
   ☐ c. special shoes.

3. Jumping from the following place would *not* be called BASE jumping:
   ☐ a. the Empire State Building.
   ☐ b. a helicopter.
   ☐ c. a radio station antenna.

4. The highest waterfall in the world is
   ☐ a. Victoria Falls in Africa.
   ☐ b. Niagara Falls between the United States and Canada.
   ☐ c. Angel Falls in Venezuela.

5. Alf Humphries's parachute caused his accident by
   ☐ a. not opening all the way.
   ☐ b. opening too soon.
   ☐ c. failing to open at all.

Score 5 points for each correct answer.

_____ **Total Score:** Recalling Facts

C | Making Inferences

When you combine your own experience and information from a text to draw a conclusion that is not directly stated in that text, you are making an inference. Below are five statements that may or may not be inferences based on information in the article. Label the statements using the following key:

C—Correct Inference   F—Faulty Inference

_____ 1. BASE jumpers who jump off the Royal Gorge Bridge do not have much respect for the laws of Colorado.

_____ 2. A truly skilled BASE jumper probably doesn't need a friend or partner nearby.

_____ 3. The U.S. government tries to protect its citizens, even from themselves.

_____ 4. If police find out about an accident in which someone dies, they usually investigate its causes.

_____ 5. If you are an experienced BASE jumper, you can be sure that your next jump will be successful and safe.

> Score 5 points for each correct answer.
>
> _____ **Total Score:** Making Inferences

D | Using Words Precisely

Each numbered sentence below contains an underlined word or phrase from the article. Following the sentence are three definitions. One definition is closest to the meaning of the underlined word. One definition is opposite or nearly opposite. Label those two definitions using the following key; do not label the remaining definition.

C—Closest   O—Opposite or Nearly Opposite

1. Then, to the <u>astonishment</u> of everyone in the church, he jumped.

_____ a. indifference

_____ b. surprise

_____ c. applause

2. In their opinion, the risk of a bloody nose or a scraped knee isn't enough to make a sport "<u>extreme</u>."

_____ a. extraordinary

_____ b. normal

_____ c. fun

3. In fact, the sport is so dangerous it is <u>banned</u> throughout the United States.

_____ a. forbidden

_____ b. talked about

_____ c. encouraged

4. It's definitely an <u>underground</u> thing.

_____ a. frightening

_____ b. open and obvious

_____ c. secret or hidden

5. The term *BASE* refers to the objects these people jump from: *B*uildings, *A*ntennae, bridge *S*pans, and other *E*arthbound objects.

_____ a. floating in space

_____ b. tall

_____ c. located on or held to the earth

_____ Score 3 points for each correct C answer.

_____ Score 2 points for each correct O answer.

_____ **Total Score:** Using Words Precisely

Enter the four total scores in the spaces below, and add them together to find your Reading Comprehension Score. Then record your score on the graph on page 149.

Score	Question Type	Lesson 14
_____	Finding the Main Idea	
_____	Recalling Facts	
_____	Making Inferences	
_____	Using Words Precisely	
_____	**Reading Comprehension Score**	

Author's Approach

Put an X in the box next to the correct answer.

1. The authors use the first sentence of the article to

☐ a. describe the setting of a BASE jumping incident.

☐ b. describe the qualities of a typical BASE jumper.

☐ c. compare BASE jumping in 1990 and BASE jumping today.

2. In this article, "Alf Humphries was 49 when he made his last jump" means

☐ a. Alf Humphries was forced to give up BASE jumping after an accident that happened when he was 49 years old.

☐ b. Alf Humphries died at the age of 49 in a BASE jumping accident.

☐ c. police officials forbade Alf Humphries from BASE jumping ever again after a terrible accident that happened when he was 49.

3. The authors emphasize how dangerous BASE jumping is. Choose the statement below that best explains how the authors address the opposing point of view in the article.

☐ a. The authors tell about the experiences of people who have died or have been injured in BASE jumping accidents.

☐ b. The authors compare BASE jumping to mountain biking and in-line skating.

☐ c. The authors quote BASE jumping fans who don't think their sport is any more dangerous than many other sports.

_____ Number of correct answers

Record your personal assessment of your work on the Critical Thinking Chart on page 150.

Summarizing and Paraphrasing

Follow the directions provided for question 1. Put an X in the box next to the correct answer for the other questions.

1. Look for the important ideas and events in paragraphs 9 and 10. Summarize those paragraphs in one or two sentences.

_____

_____

_____

2. Read the statement from the article below. Then read the paraphrase of that statement. Choose the reason that best tells why the paraphrase does not say the same thing as the statement.

   Statement: BASE jumpers should double-check their parachutes before a jump to be sure that they work properly.

   Paraphrase: It is essential for BASE jumpers to double-check their equipment; a properly working parachute can mean the difference between life and death.

   ☐ a. Paraphrase says too much.

   ☐ b. Paraphrase doesn't say enough.

   ☐ c. Paraphrase doesn't agree with the statement.

3. Choose the best one-sentence paraphrase for the following sentence from the article: "[BASE jumping] is definitely an underground thing."

   ☐ a. BASE jumpers have begun jumping in underground caves.

   ☐ b. BASE jumping is a sport that is usually enjoyed in secret.

   ☐ c. BASE jumping is becoming a popular, mainstream sport.

_____ Number of correct answers

Record your personal assessment of your work on the Critical Thinking Chart on page 150.

Critical Thinking

Put an X in the box next to the correct answer for questions 1 and 2. Follow the directions provided for the other questions.

1. Which of the following statements from the article is an opinion rather than a fact?

   ☐ a. [BASE jumping] is just like any other sport.

   ☐ b. As the man floated to the floor, he almost hit a woman.

   ☐ c. More than 30 BASE jumpers have died since the sport began.

2. From what Scott Chew said, you can predict that if Alf Humphries carefully explained to him why he shouldn't BASE jump, Chew would

   ☐ a. accuse Humphries of being a coward.

   ☐ b. listen to his friend and stop BASE jumping for good.

   ☐ c. ignore the advice of his friend and continue to BASE jump.

3. Using what you know about parachuting and what is told about BASE jumping in the article, name three ways BASE jumping is similar to and three ways BASE jumping is different from normal parachuting. Cite the paragraph number(s) where you found details in the article to support your conclusions.

Similarities

_____

_____

_____

Differences

_____

_____

_____

_____

4. Choose from the letters below to correctly complete the following statement. Write the letters on the lines.

    According to the article, _____ caused Alf Humphries to _____, and the effect was _____.

    a. hit the ground and break his spine

    b. Alf Humphries will spend the rest of his life in a wheelchair

    c. the failure of Alf Humphries's parachute to open

5. In which paragraph did you find your information or details to answer question 4? _____

_____ Number of correct answers

Record your personal assessment of your work on the Critical Thinking Chart on page 150.

Personal Response

Would you recommend this article to other students? Explain.

_____

_____

_____

_____

Self-Assessment

One of the things I did best when reading this article was _____

_____.

I believe I did this well because _____

_____

_____

_____

Raid Gauloises: 10 Days of Hell

First you are climbing the walls of a huge canyon as water from a waterfall pounds on your head. Then you are kayaking through shark-filled waters with a storm raging all around you. Next you are riding a camel across a desert with sand blowing in your face and the sun beating down on your back. Are you trapped in some kind of bad dream? No, but that's close. You are in the Raid Gauloises, a grueling 10-day race that takes people to the edge of death.

Contestants in the Raid Gauloises must be ready for anything! This team is riding horseback through the Pampas Lindas on the fourth leg of the race, which was held in Patagonia, Argentina.

2   The Raid Gauloises (pronounced *rād•gō•lowahz*) started in 1989. A Frenchman named Gérard Fusil set it up. Fusil wanted a race that would lead people through the wildest lands left on Earth. He wanted racers to stretch themselves beyond all human limits. He wanted them to cover huge distances and face many dangers. In return, winners would receive thousands of dollars in prize money. But more than that, they would have the joy of knowing they survived the toughest course Mother Nature could offer.

3   Fusil set up simple rules for the race. Athletes must compete in groups of five. At least one person in each group must be a woman. And, in order to win, the entire team has to make it to the finish line. If one person drops out, the whole team is disqualified.

4   Teams have 10 days to complete five legs, or stages, of the race. Each leg requires different skills. One leg might involve rock climbing. Another might include parachuting off a mountain. A third might call for white-water rafting, long-distance running, or mountain biking.

5   To keep the race fresh, Fusil decided it should be held in a different place each year. Racers are told the general location months in advance. But they don't know the exact route until 24 hours before race time. Then they are given maps showing the starting and finish lines of each leg. The maps also show the checkpoints the teams must pass through. Otherwise, the course is not marked. There are no aid stations along the way and no trails to follow. So each team is truly on its own. The only help comes in the form of rescue helicopters. Teams carry flares that they can shoot off if they want a helicopter to come get them. But since that means dropping out of the race, flares are always a last resort.

6   In 1990 the Raid Gauloises was held in Costa Rica. Athletes had to race through jungles thick with poisonous snakes. They had to hike miles through alligator country. They had to contend with sweltering heat, endless beds of loose sand, and the constant threat of panther attacks.

7   In 1992 the race was set in the Arab country of Oman. Here, athletes had to watch out for scorpions. They had to deal with jellyfish and leeches. They ran the risk of getting malaria and heatstroke. The 1994 race took place in Borneo. The jungles were so thick that it was hard to get through them. One U.S. team got lost in the tangled overgrowth. The team wandered for 24 hours before finally finding its way out.

8   Despite the punishing nature of the race, it is a big success. In 1995, 48 teams from around the world came to compete in it. This time the setting was Patagonia, an area of southern Argentina. As always, "Raiders" were warned of the problems they would face. The temperature could range from 20°–110° F. There would be snow in the mountains and ice in the lakes. Yet during the day, the sun would be very hot. Athletes were urged to use their sunscreen, even on their lips. Otherwise, said one race official, "your lips will swell up like huge tomatoes."

9   When the race began, the teams took off across a lake in sea kayaks. They had to paddle 31 miles in strong winds. Everyone made it through this first leg. But the second leg was harder. The athletes had to climb up a huge,

jagged mountain called Mount Tronador. The sun beat down without mercy. One woman became sick and couldn't stop vomiting. One climber hurt his knee and saw it puff up to the size of a grapefruit. Meanwhile, a French team got lost. They spent nine hours struggling to get back on course.

10   As the hours slipped by, all the Raiders grew weary. Yet they were reluctant to stop. They knew that each minute they rested, they were losing ground to some other team. Besides, the idea of camping in the snow without sleeping bags was not very appealing. On the other hand, climbing in the dark was no picnic, either. One woman broke her leg doing that. Another man's hand was crushed by a rock that fell in the dark.

11   Those who kept going eventually found themselves surrounded by ice. To get to the top of Mount Tronador, the members of each team had to rope themselves together. That was the only way to be sure they didn't slip off, fall off, or blow off the mountain.

12   By this time, the athletes were in their fourth full day of racing. They were exhausted. They staggered along with their backs bent and their eyes sunk in. Some had frostbite on their feet. One man started hallucinating. Another developed pneumonia. Many were badly burned by the sun. Writer David Tracey, who followed the progress of the athletes, noted that "one [American] racer . . . is suffering from a sunburned tongue. He does not want to talk about it."

13   By the end of the mountain stage, more than 10 teams had dropped out. The rest were struggling to hang on. "This mountain made me cry," said French Raider Isabelle Mir as she came down off Mount Tronador. "I've never suffered so much physically and mentally." Yet she and many others pushed on to the canoeing stage. Here, teams had to fight their way through white-water rapids. In places, they had to leave the water and carry their canoes for miles through bamboo forests. A Spanish team, made up of all women, finished this bruising 40-mile leg in just 30 hours. They did it without taking a single break along the way.

14   The fourth stage required teams to complete a long, hard ride on horseback. Several riders were thrown from their horses, but they climbed back on and kept going. The final stage was a walk-run-climb through canyons and forests. An Austrian team lost its map in this section. They began to wander around in desperation. Luckily, they found a French team that offered to share its map with them.

15   Many people might think those who compete in the Raid Gauloises are just plain nuts. But don't try to tell that to the athletes who have done it. For them, Raid Gauloises is the ultimate challenge in the world of sports.

If you have been timed while reading this article, enter your reading time below. Then turn to the Words-per-Minute table on page 147 and look up your reading speed (words per minute). Enter your reading speed on the graph on page 148.

Reading Time: Lesson 15

_____ : _____
Minutes   *Seconds*

A | Finding the Main Idea

One statement below expresses the main idea of the article. One statement is too general, or too broad. The other statement explains only part of the article; it is too narrow. Label the statements using the following key:

M—Main Idea   B—Too Broad   N—Too Narrow

_____ 1. The Raid Gauloises was started in 1989 by a Frenchman named Gérard Fusil.

_____ 2. Perhaps the most extreme of extreme sports is the Raid Gauloises.

_____ 3. The Raid Gauloises, a 10-day race held each year in wild lands, tests athletes under the most trying conditions.

_____ Score 15 points for a correct M answer.

_____ Score 5 points for each correct B or N answer.

_____ **Total Score:** Finding the Main Idea

B | Recalling Facts

How well do you remember the facts in the article? Put an X in the box next to the answer that correctly completes each statement about the article.

1. Each five-member team must include at least
   ☐ a. one woman.
   ☐ b. one French citizen.
   ☐ c. one professional athlete.

2. If one member of a team drops out,
   ☐ a. the team uses a flare to notify officials.
   ☐ b. the rest of the team must call in a substitute.
   ☐ c. the whole team is disqualified.

3. The teams are guided through the course by
   ☐ a. signs and guideposts spaced one mile apart.
   ☐ b. a map showing the starting and finish lines of each leg, and checkpoints along the way.
   ☐ c. radio signals broadcast from the finish line of each leg.

4. Skills needed in past Raid Gauloises events include
   ☐ a. fishing for sharks and figure skating.
   ☐ b. pitching, catching, and fielding.
   ☐ c. rock climbing, kayaking, and biking.

5. During the 1994 race in Borneo, one U.S. team
   ☐ a. was lost in the jungle for a day.
   ☐ b. won the event by a full day.
   ☐ c. got lost and was never seen again.

Score 5 points for each correct answer.

_____ **Total Score:** Recalling Facts

C Making Inferences

When you combine your own experience and information from a text to draw a conclusion that is not directly stated in that text, you are making an inference. Below are five statements that may or may not be inferences based on information in the article. Label the statements using the following key:

C—Correct Inference   F—Faulty Inference

_____ 1. Before each race, the members of each team find out about every hazard along the route.

_____ 2. Countries are eager to host the race because being chosen proves that the country is a good place for tourists to visit.

_____ 3. Gérard Fusil would be unhappy if newspapers and television networks sent huge news teams to cover the Raid Gauloises and set up news centers along each leg of the race.

_____ 4 A smart investor would put money into a resort for beginning mountain climbers at the foot of Mount Tronador.

_____ 5. It is possible for an all-woman team to win the Raid Gauloises.

Score 5 points for each correct answer.

_____ **Total Score:** Making Inferences

D Using Words Precisely

Each numbered sentence below contains an underlined word or phrase from the article. Following the sentence are three definitions. One definition is closest to the meaning of the underlined word. One definition is opposite or nearly opposite. Label those two definitions using the following key; do not label the remaining definition.

C—Closest   O—Opposite or Nearly Opposite

1. If one person drops out, the whole team is <u>disqualified</u>.

_____ a. allowed to compete

_____ b. popular

_____ c. no longer allowed to win

2. Then they are given maps showing the starting and finish lines of each <u>leg</u>.

_____ a. one section among several

_____ b. whole

_____ c. program

3. But since that means dropping out of the race, flares are always a last <u>resort</u>.

_____ a. obstacle

_____ b. plan

_____ c. place to turn to for help

4. As the hours slipped by, all the Raiders grew weary. Yet they were <u>reluctant</u> to stop.

_____ a. late

_____ b. eager

_____ c. hesitant

5. They <u>staggered</u> along with their backs bent and their eyes sunk in.

_____ a. worked

_____ b. strode

_____ c. tottered

_____ Score 3 points for each correct C answer.

_____ Score 2 points for each correct O answer.

_____ **Total Score:** Using Words Precisely

Enter the four total scores in the spaces below, and add them together to find your Reading Comprehension Score. Then record your score on the graph on page 149.

Score	Question Type	Lesson 15
_____	Finding the Main Idea	
_____	Recalling Facts	
_____	Making Inferences	
_____	Using Words Precisely	
_____	**Reading Comprehension Score**	

Author's Approach

Put an X in the box next to the correct answer.

1. The main purpose of the first paragraph is to

☐ a. express an opinion about Raid Gauloises.

☐ b. exaggerate the dangers of the Raid Gauloises.

☐ c. describe a typical day in the Raid Gauloises.

2. What is the authors' purpose in writing "Raid Gauloises: 10 Days of Hell"?

☐ a. to encourage the reader to participate in the Raid Gauloises

☐ b. to inform the reader about the Raid Gauloises

☐ d. to emphasize the similarities between Raid Gauloises and other races

3. Judging by statements from the article, you can conclude that the authors want the reader to think that

☐ a. the Raid Gauloises is unfair to women.

☐ b. just making it to the finish line in the Raid Gauloises is a personal triumph.

☐ c. the Raid Gauloises is dangerous and should be stopped.

4. What do the authors imply by saying "Several riders were thrown from their horses, but they climbed back on and kept going"?

☐ a. The horses used in this race were trained to be unruly.

☐ b. The athletes in the race were poor horse handlers.

☐ c. The riders were brave and determined.

_____ Number of correct answers

Record your personal assessment of your work on the Critical Thinking Chart on page 150.

Summarizing and Paraphrasing

Follow the directions provided for question 1. Put an X in the box next to the correct answer for the other questions.

1. Complete the following one-sentence summary of the article using the lettered phrases from the phrase bank below. Write the letters on the lines.

    > **Phrase Bank**
    > a. how the race is organized and run
    > b. the origin of the Raid Gauloises
    > c. a description of the phases of the 10-day race

    The article "Raid Gauloises: 10 Days of Hell" begins with

    _____, goes on to explain _____, and ends with

    _____.

2. Below are summaries of the article. Choose the summary that says all the most important things about the article but in the fewest words.

    ☐ a. The Raid Gauloises, a strenuous 10-day race held in a different place each year, consists of five stages. Each stage demands a particular physical skill.

    ☐ b. The place where the Raid Gauloises is held each year determines the skills that the racers will need. For example, in Costa Rica, athletes had to race through jungles and withstand extreme heat. In Patagonia, however, racers needed to paddle across a windy lake and deal with frostbite on a huge mountain.

    ☐ c. The athletes who participate in the Raid Gauloises are eager to prove themselves in a variety of sports. Each team must have at least one woman.

3. Choose the sentence that correctly restates the following sentence from the article: "Despite the punishing nature of the race, it is a big success."

    ☐ a. The race punishes nature, though it is also successful.

    ☐ b. Even though the race is successful, people punish it.

    ☐ c. Although the race is grueling, it is quite popular.

    > _____ Number of correct answers
    >
    > Record your personal assessment of your work on the Critical Thinking Chart on page 150.

Critical Thinking

Follow the directions provided for question 1. Put an X in the box next to the correct answer for the other questions.

1. For each statement below, write *O* if it expresses an opinion or write *F* if it expresses a fact.

    _____ a. The athletes who participate in the Raid Gauloises don't value their lives properly; they take foolish chances for no good reason.

    _____ b. It is a good idea to require each team in the Raid Gauloises to have at least one woman.

    _____ c. The Raid Gauloises started in 1989.

2. From what the article told about the Raid Gauloises, you can predict that

☐ a. next year, the race will be held in the same place it was held this year.

☐ b. next year, the race will be held in a different place from where it was held this year.

☐ c. next year about one month ahead of the start of the race, officials will give out maps showing the starting and finish lines as well as the checkpoints.

3. How is the Raid Gauloises an example of an extreme sport?

☐ a. To participate in the Raid Gauloises, you need to be in excellent physical condition.

☐ b. The Raid Gauloises is held in many different places around the world, each one offering its own set of dangers and thrills.

☐ c. Successful completion of Raid Gauloises demands unusual strength and skill; Raid Gauloises is quite dangerous.

4. If you were an athlete hoping to enter next year's Raid Gauloises, how could you best use the information in the article to prepare for the race?

☐ a. Train in a wide variety of sports, after studying the sports that have been featured in previous races.

☐ b. Train in running at high altitudes.

☐ c. Try to guess where the race will be next year, and train in sports that will probably be featured there.

5. What did you have to do to answer question 1?

☐ a. find a fact (something that you can prove is true)

☐ b. find a description (how something looks)

☐ c. find a cause (why something happened)

_____ Number of correct answers

Record your personal assessment of your work on the Critical Thinking Chart on page 150.

Personal Response

If I were the authors, I would add _____

_____

because _____

_____

Self-Assessment

While reading the article, I found it easiest to _____

_____

_____

_____

_____

Compare and Contrast

Think about the articles you have read in Unit Three. Pick the three most unusual sports. Write the titles of the articles that tell about them in the first column of the chart below. Use information you learned from the articles to fill in the empty boxes in the chart.

Title	What equipment does an athlete in this sport use?	How does an athlete know when he or she has been successful?	Why would an athlete participate in this sport?

If I could ask one question of a participant in this sport, _____, it would be

_____

_____

Words-per-Minute Table

Unit Three

Directions: If you were timed while reading an article, refer to the Reading Time you recorded in the box at the end of the article. Use this words-per-minute table to determine your reading speed for that article. Then plot your reading speed on the graph on page 148.

Lesson / No. of Words	11 / 1,065	12 / 1,048	13 / 1,022	14 / 939	15 / 1,140	Seconds
1:30	710	699	681	626	760	90
1:40	639	629	613	563	684	100
1:50	581	572	557	512	622	110
2:00	533	524	511	470	570	120
2:10	492	484	472	433	526	130
2:20	456	449	438	402	489	140
2:30	426	419	409	376	456	150
2:40	399	393	383	352	428	160
2:50	376	370	361	331	402	170
3:00	355	349	341	313	380	180
3:10	336	331	323	297	360	190
3:20	320	314	307	282	342	200
3:30	304	299	292	268	326	210
3:40	290	286	279	256	311	220
3:50	278	273	267	245	297	230
4:00	266	262	256	235	285	240
4:10	256	252	245	225	274	250
4:20	246	242	236	217	263	260
4:30	237	233	227	209	253	270
4:40	228	225	219	201	244	280
4:50	220	217	211	194	236	290
5:00	213	210	204	188	228	300
5:10	206	203	198	182	221	310
5:20	200	197	192	176	214	320
5:30	194	191	186	171	207	330
5:40	188	185	180	166	201	340
5:50	183	180	175	161	195	350
6:00	178	175	170	157	190	360
6:10	173	170	166	152	185	370
6:20	168	165	161	148	180	380
6:30	164	161	157	144	175	390
6:40	160	157	153	141	171	400
6:50	156	153	150	137	167	410
7:00	152	150	146	134	163	420
7:10	149	146	143	131	159	430
7:20	145	143	139	128	155	440
7:30	142	140	136	125	152	450
7:40	139	137	133	122	149	460
7:50	136	134	130	120	146	470
8:00	133	131	128	117	143	480

Minutes and Seconds

Plotting Your Progress: Reading Speed

Unit Three

Directions: If you were timed while reading an article, write your words-per-minute rate for that article in the box under the number of the lesson. Then plot your reading speed on the graph by putting a small X on the line directly above the number of the lesson, across from the number of words per minute you read. As you mark your speed for each lesson, graph your progress by drawing a line to connect the X's.

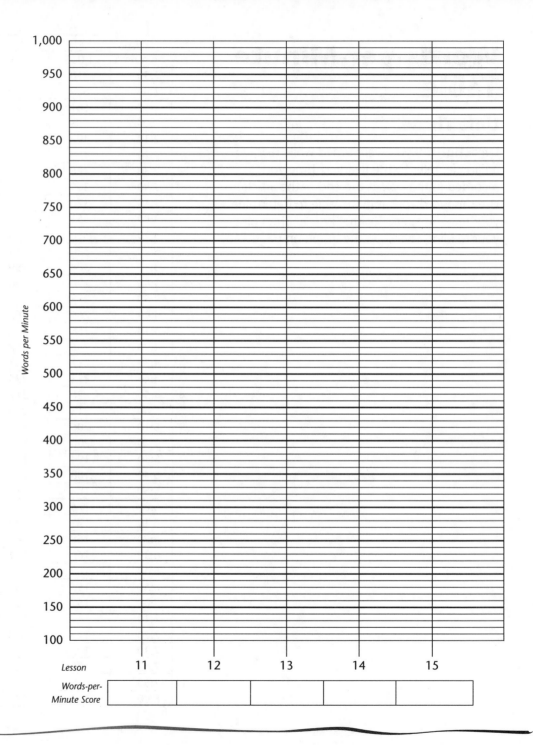

Plotting Your Progress: Reading Comprehension

Unit Three

Directions: Write your Reading Comprehension Score for each lesson in the box under the number of the lesson. Then plot your score on the graph by putting a small X on the line directly above the number of the lesson and across from the score you earned. As you mark your score for each lesson, graph your progress by drawing a line to connect the X's.

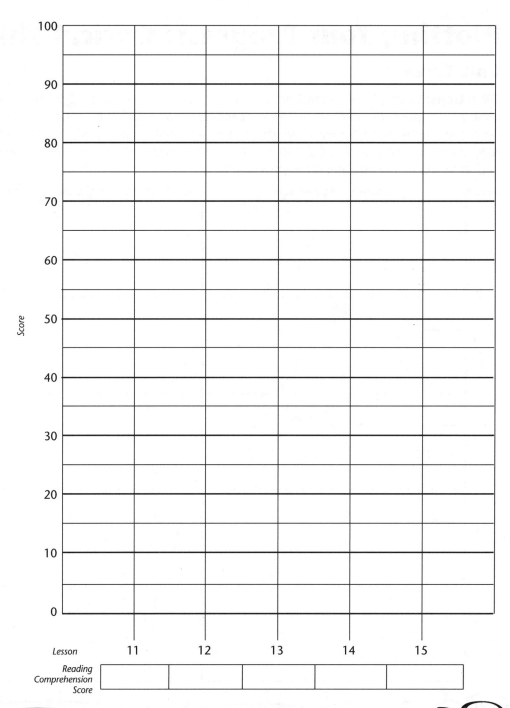

Plotting Your Progress: Critical Thinking

Unit Three

Directions: Work with your teacher to evaluate your responses to the Critical Thinking questions for each lesson. Then fill in the appropriate spaces in the chart below. For each lesson and each type of Critical Thinking question, do the following: Mark a minus sign (–) in the box to indicate areas in which you feel you could improve. Mark a plus sign (+) to indicate areas in which you feel you did well. Mark a minus-slash-plus sign (–/+) to indicate areas in which you had mixed success. Then write any comments you have about your performance, including ideas for improvement.

Lesson	Author's Approach	Summarizing and Paraphrasing	Critical Thinking
11			
12			
13			
14			
15			

Photo Credits

Sample Lesson: pp. 3, 4 Reneé Vernon and Adventure Photo & Film

Unit 1 Opener: p. 13 D. Gorton/The New York Times

Lesson 1: p. 14 Doug Berry/Telluride Stock Photography

Lesson 2: p. 22 AP/Wide World Photos

Lesson 3: p. 30 American River Touring Association

Lesson 4: p. 38 D. Gorton/The New York Times

Lesson 5: p. 46 AP/Wide World Photos

Unit 2 Opener: p. 59 The Image Bank

Lesson 6: p. 60 Mike Hewitt/Allsport USA

Lesson 7: p. 68 Gary Sanders Breitnacher/Adventure Photo & Film

Lesson 8: p. 76 real Cecile/Gamma-Liaison Network

Lesson 9: p. 84 Bettman/Corbis

Lesson 10: p. 92 The Image Bank

Unit 3 Opener: p. 105 The Image Bank

Lesson 11: p. 106 Hulton Getty Picture Library/Archive Photos

Lesson 12: p. 114 Mike Powell/Allsport USA

Lesson 13: p. 122 The Image Bank

Lesson 14: p. 130 Tom Sanders/Adventure Photo & Film

Lesson 15: p. 138 Tony Di Zinno/Libero Di Zinno Photographs